Effective Practices in Workplace Language Training

Guidelines for Providers of Workplace English Language Training Services

Joan Friedenberg
Deborah Kennedy
Anne Lomperis
William Martin
Kay Westerfield

With contributions from Margaret van Naerssen

TESOL Teachers of English to Speakers of Other Languages, Inc.

Typeset in Bodoni and Novarese Display
by Capitol Communications Systems, Inc., Crofton, Maryland USA
Printed by Kirby Lithographic Company, Inc. USA

Teachers of English to Speakers of Other Languages, Inc.
700 South Washington Street, Suite 200
Alexandria, Virginia 22314 USA
Tel 703-836-0774 • Fax 703-836-6447 • E-mail info@tesol.org • http://www.tesol.org/

Director of Communications and Marketing: Helen Kornblum
Editor: Deborah Kennedy
Additional Reader: Marcia Annis
Cover Design: Capitol Communications Systems, Inc.

ISBN 193118500X
LCCN 2001 135520

Table of Contents

Introduction

Definition of Effective Practices

The word *practices*, as used in this book, refers to the processes and strategies that a workplace English language training provider follows in developing, providing, and evaluating language programs and services. *Effective practices* in workplace English language training are those processes and strategies that lead to excellence, as documented in real training situations. Effective practices are not only better by comparison with other ways of operating; they stand on their own as models to be emulated.

Effective practices in workplace English language training lead to optimal outcomes for all stakeholders. For employees who participate in language training, those outcomes include improved language skills, increased job satisfaction, enhanced self-esteem, greater job mobility, and higher earning potential. For employers, optimal outcomes manifest themselves as return on investment, measured in terms of increases in productivity, work quality, and positive worker attitudes and decreases in employee turnover, errors and misunderstandings, accidents, and absenteeism. For language training providers, optimal outcomes include enhanced capability, broader professional recognition, and increased profitability.

As processes and strategies, effective practices illustrate the *how* of workplace English language training. Each effective practice describes the way in which a training provider behaves with respect to one aspect of the development, provision, and evaluation of its programs and services, and each is composed of a series of subprocesses or steps that characterize what a provider does and how it does it. These effective practices and their constituent steps thus can serve as benchmarks or points of reference against which workplace language training providers can compare their own ways of operating.

Audience and Purpose

This book is intended primarily for workplace language training providers, although corporations and organizations wishing to employ such providers' services will also find the discussion useful. The purpose of this book is to promote quality and accountability among providers of workplace English language training programs and thus enable providers and client organizations to recognize the essential elements of workplace language training and develop realistic expectations for provider relationships and program outcomes.

This book enables new and experienced providers of workplace English language training programs to recognize and implement the processes that will result in optimal outcomes for all involved. The practices outlined in the text and illustrated with case studies drawn from successful English language training situations can serve as guidelines for workplace language trainers and program administrators as they plan, deliver, and evaluate workplace language training.

For corporations and organizations that currently use or intend to use the services of a workplace language training provider, this book provides insight into the necessary components of a quality workplace English language training program. The practices outlined in the text can help client organizations set realistic expectations and ensure that they are obtaining quality workplace language training for participating employees.

This book gives a coordinated, knowledgeable response at the international level to the design, delivery, and evaluation of workplace language training programs while, at the same time, recognizing that those programs exist in a wide variety of settings. It thus addresses the needs of English as a second language (ESL) situations, where employees must use English in most, if not all, contexts, and English as a foreign language (EFL) situations, where employees use English only for specific workplace or business purposes. Although the cases and examples in the text relate to English language training in the workplace, the practices may also be useful for training in languages other than English, that is, for the broader field of language for occupational purposes (LOP).

◼ Myths and Facts About Workplace English Language Training

Workplace language training providers frequently encounter misconceptions about the nature of the profession. The four that follow are the most common of these.

Myth 1: Every English language course is really an English for specific purposes (ESP) training program.

Fact: Every well-designed language course takes into consideration the needs of the learners and has clear learning objectives and appropriate materials, methodology, and evaluation procedures. However, because learners in an ESP situation have more specific and definable needs, ESP programs need to be more focused than general English courses. English for occupational purposes (EOP) programs, in particular, need to be built on knowledge of the workplace because participants have clear, often urgent work-related needs and goals.

Myth 2: EOP is simply memorizing technical vocabulary.

Fact: EOP involves much more than memorizing long lists of technical terminology. It is not learning about a task, but learning how to do the task in the target language. This requires consideration of all areas of communicative competence, and is far more complex than just lists of technical vocabulary.

Myth 3: Just use this textbook, and you will have a great EOP program.

Fact: An EOP program does not start with the text and let that drive the course. EOP is based on a needs assessment that specifies exactly what the learner has to do in the target language and employs actual workplace texts and tasks to teach it. Published materials or parts thereof may or may not be appropriate, depending on the results of the needs assessment. EOP programs by definition are not off-the-shelf.

Myth 4: Anyone who teaches can develop and teach an EOP training program.

Fact: EOP is a training specialty. To develop and teach a workplace language program that effectively meets the needs of participating employees and their employers, a provider should be grounded in the theory and practice of adult language learning and teaching, including needs assessment, curriculum and materials development, and teaching and learning styles. The effective practices described in this book illustrate the provider qualifications that form the foundation for successful workplace language training.

▮ Theoretical Basis of the Approach Profiled in This Volume

Needs assessment and authenticity in tasks and materials provide the theoretical foundation for workplace language training. The approach profiled in this volume is based, in addition, on three developments in the theory of second language learning and teaching: language acquisition, communicative competence, and task-based instruction. These are not the only theoretical bases for language instruction (see Peyton & Crandall, 1995), but they underlie many effective workplace language training programs.

Language Acquisition

Movements in foreign and second language teaching and research (including Krashen, 1982) have reinforced the ESP principle of designing language learning activities around real purposes that involve the exchange of information and moving away from activities that accomplish only the artificial purpose of producing the correct grammatical form. In workplace English language training programs, this means using real (or realistic) workplace materials and situations and emphasizing pair and small-group interaction rather than individual drilling and repetition. This approach allows learners to focus on learning the language instead of merely learning about it, and enables instructors to target error correction specifically to matters that may interfere with the performance of work-related communication.

Communicative Competence

The idea that the goal of language acquisition is *communicative competence*, that is, the ability to use the language correctly and appropriately to accomplish communication goals, was first put forth by Hymes (1971) and has subsequently been refined and applied to a variety of teaching contexts (see, e.g., Savignon, 1983, 1991). In the communicative competence model, proficiency in a language goes beyond abstract knowledge about the language to encompass four types of competence: linguistic, sociolinguistic, discourse, and strategic.

1. *Linguistic competence* is the basic ability to use the grammar, syntax, and vocabulary of a language. Linguistic competence enables the speaker of a language to recognize words and the ways in which they can be used to form phrases and sentences.

2. *Sociolinguistic competence* is knowing how to use and respond to language appropriately, taking into account the social and cultural rules that govern the setting, the topic, and the role relationships of those involved in communication. Sociolinguistic competence tells the speaker of a language which words and phrases fit the setting and topic, how to express a particular attitude (e.g., courtesy, authority, friendliness, respect), and how to recognize the attitude another person is expressing.

3. *Discourse competence* is knowing how to interpret sentences within a larger linguistic context and how to construct longer stretches of language so that the parts make up a coherent whole. Discourse competence tells the speaker of a language how words, phrases, and sentences are put together to create larger units, such as conversations, speeches, and written paragraphs.

4. *Strategic competence* is having strategies for recognizing and repairing communication breakdowns, for compensating for gaps in one's knowledge of the language, and for learning more about communication in the language and in the sociocultural context. Strategic competence informs the speaker of a language when misunderstanding has occurred and tells the speaker how to use language to remedy the situation.

In workplace English language training programs, the idea that communicative competence is the goal of language learning has led to a broadening of the content and types of activities that take place in language classrooms. Through observations, role plays, presentations, and other learner-centered activities, instructors encourage learners to develop their ability not only to produce language but to produce extended sequences of language that are appropriate to a specific context and accomplish defined communication goals.

Task-Based Instruction

In order to translate the language acquisition theory and communicative competence model outlined above into classroom practice, language instructors at many levels have turned to task-based instruction. A *task* in this context is defined as an action that is accomplished through the use of language. It involves a function, such as introducing oneself, making an activity report, or responding to a request for information, and the conditions connected with the function, such as length, people involved, and level of advance planning. Carrying out a task involves using some or all of the four language modalities together to comprehend and produce meaningful communication (Nunan, 1989).

Task-based instruction is effective in workplace settings because it allows a training program to address the language skills learners need for specific work situations and to structure the syllabus to reflect a series of such situations. The instructor acts as a model and guide, presenting task-related language and then providing support as learners work in pairs or small groups to complete activities using that language.

Task-based instruction is effective at all levels of language proficiency; the tasks are keyed to learners' workplace needs and skill levels (Oxford, 2001). For example, for the topic of workplace safety where English is the language of the workplace, learners at lower language skill levels might do pair role plays in which a longtime employee gives basic safety precautions (e.g., "Always wear your hardhat") to a new one, and then work in groups to create basic safety posters for the workplace. Learners at more advanced levels might give individual or pair presentations on aspects of safety.

Adult Learning Theory and Learner-Centered Instruction

The approach profiled in this volume also builds on several principles of adult learning theory that have gained currency since the 1960s.

- Adults need to be involved in the planning and evaluation of their instruction.

- Adults are most interested in learning subjects that have immediate relevance to their jobs or personal lives.

- Adult learning is problem centered rather than content oriented.

- Experience, including mistakes, provides the basis for learning.

These principles have led to the development of learner-centered instruction, an approach used by many effective training providers. In this approach, learners participate actively in every class session, developing and practicing language skills as they work together in teams or pairs on specific communication tasks and problems. The instructor models linguistic, sociolinguistic, discourse, and strategic competence at key points, then serves as a resource for learners as they practice the language themselves. Activities include role plays, group projects, and collaborative writing, and learners contribute to the curriculum by bringing communication challenges they have encountered in the workplace to class for discussion.

For example, in programs with a focus on oral communication, participants may role play interactions with coworkers and customers, practice turn-taking or initiating a topic in meetings, or make simulated sales presentations with videotaping for later review. In programs that focus on writing, participants may work in pairs to compare their writing styles to that of a model business document. All of these activities engage participants in authentic practice of work-related communication tasks.

Learner-centered instruction is effective because it enables participants to build on the knowledge and experience they already possess and encourages them to take responsibility for their own learning. By providing authentic opportunities for practice and problem solving, it simulates the real workplace, where employees must communicate and solve communication problems on their own. In this way, learner-centered instruction promotes the transfer of skills and knowledge from the classroom to the workplace.

▰ The Role of Workplace Language Training in Human Resources Management and Public Policy

Executives and human resources managers who seek to make the most of available resources recognize employees as a company's human capital. The knowledge, skills, and other inherent qualities that employees possess are resources that contribute to the well-being of employees, the company for which they work, and their nation as a whole.

In assessing the economic impact of language skills, Chiswick (1996) notes that proficiency in the language of commerce, instruction, and government meets the three key requirements of human capital.

1. "It is embodied in the person" (p. 3): Language skills cannot be taken away from a person, unlike a tractor or tool.

2. "It is costly to create" (p. 3): Developing language skills requires an investment of time and (often) money.

3. "It is productive" (p. 3): Individuals, companies, and the national economy can see a return on this investment in the form of increased productivity in the labor market and improved quality of life.

Workplace language training gives companies a mechanism for increasing this essential form of human capital. Such training improves employment and earnings opportunities for employees as it increases their potential for contributing to the success of the company. Further, Chiswick (1996) notes, language training has a positive effect on "the aggregate human capital available to the economy" (p. 2).

This potential for high-level economic impact underscores the value of workplace language training programs. To achieve the greatest positive effect, however, workplace language training providers must continually strive to improve their services and programs. The effective practices described in this book illustrate approaches and methods that characterize such quality workplace language training providers.

Overview of Effective Practices in Workplace Language Training

The effective practices are organized into nine groups, with three to five subpractices under each major practice. Though necessary for topical reasons, this structure presents a potentially misleading sense of linearity. In fact, the process of establishing a relationship with a client, conducting needs assessments, designing and developing a training program, and evaluating outcomes is highly iterative. Provider and client often refine their understanding of needs as training, and the formative evaluation that accompanies it, proceed. In other words, the process of setting up and sustaining a workplace language training program is not linear, but overlapping and ongoing.

Effective Practice 1: The workplace language training provider has an effective, current strategic plan

Practice 1.1:   articulate mission and values

Practice 1.2:   identify internal strengths and weaknesses

Practice 1.3:   analyze external opportunities and threats

Practice 1.4:   set goals and create development and marketing strategies

Effective Practice 2: The workplace language training provider conducts effective marketing activities

Practice 2.1:   understand the target market

Practice 2.2:   educate the target market

Practice 2.3:   develop effective, appropriate marketing materials and techniques

Practice 2.4:   maintain a positive public image

▰ *Effective Practice* 3: The workplace language training provider builds a strong client relationship in conducting an organizational needs assessment and developing a proposed program and contract

Practice 3.1:   establish a relationship of mutual respect and trust

Practice 3.2:   determine client needs, expectations, and goals

Practice 3.3:   design a program

Practice 3.4:   prepare and submit a proposal

Practice 3.5:   negotiate the contract

▰ *Effective Practice* 4: The workplace language training provider provides quality program staff and appropriate staff support

Practice 4.1:   determine necessary staffing level and administrative structure of the program

Practice 4.2:   recruit and select qualified staff

Practice 4.3:   provide appropriate and effective staff support and development

▰ *Effective Practice* 5: The workplace language training provider conducts a comprehensive research-based instructional needs assessment

Practice 5.1:   define the rationale and framework for the assessment

Practice 5.2:   involve all stakeholders in the assessment process

Practice 5.3:   collect and analyze data on language use in the workplace

Practice 5.4:   collect data on the oral and written language proficiency of (potential) participants

Practice 5.5:   report the results of the instructional needs assessment to the client

▰ *Effective Practice* 6: The workplace language training provider creates a flexible, research-based instructional design

Practice 6.1:   translate program goals and instructional needs assessment into initial performance objectives

Practice 6.2:   conduct a communication task/language analysis (CT/LA) for each task or topic area listed in the performance objectives

Practice 6.3:   on the basis of principles of language learning and client priorities, develop an appropriate framework for sequencing topics and tasks

Practice 6.4:   create an instructional schedule that accommodates participant and client needs

Practice 6.5:   produce a written course document that allows for adjustment when necessary

Effective Practice 7: The workplace language training provider develops and selects program-specific training materials and activities

Practice 7.1:   develop program-specific materials from those found in the workplace

Practice 7.2:   augment developed materials with appropriate existing materials

Practice 7.3:   plan activities that engage learners in the authentic practice of work-related language use

Practice 7.4:   plan activities that engage learners in the authentic practice of work-related language use

Practice 7.5:   plan for the appropriate use of available technology

Effective Practice 8: The workplace language training provider delivers instruction that keeps participants involved and motivated

Practice 8.1:   use appropriate language teaching approaches

Practice 8.2:   involve workplace supervisors and other staff appropriately

Practice 8.3:   conduct formative evaluation and adjust curriculum as participant or client needs become clearer or change

Practice 8.4:   monitor the training and maintain communication with the client

Practice 8.5:   provide recognition of completion to participants and recognition of contributions to client representatives

Effective Practice 9: The workplace language training provider conducts a program evaluation that relates program outcomes to program goals and serves as a guide for future training

Practice 9.1:   outline the reasons for evaluating the program

Practice 9.2:   identify an effective evaluation model

Practice 9.3:   define and implement appropriate evaluation mechanisms

Practice 9.4:   provide a written report of evaluation results and recommendations for future training

Practice 9.5:   conduct periodic follow-up

Effective Practice 1

The Workplace Language Training Provider Has an Effective, Current Strategic Plan

Overview

A successful workplace language training provider builds programs and services based upon a strategic plan that outlines what the programs and services will provide, for whom, where, how, and why. That is, the provider takes a proactive, intentional approach to developing all or a part of its own identity and function as a provider of workplace language training.

Through the systematic internal and external analysis that takes place in the strategic planning process, a provider evaluates its own potential and the business environment in which it operates. The provider is then able to articulate its distinctive competency and the assets and abilities it can offer its clients, and to describe in realistic terms what workplace language training can and cannot do. The provider is also able to think creatively about ways to identify and meet its clients' needs.

Strategic planning involves four interrelated processes. First, the provider articulates its mission and the values that motivate and guide its activities. In the second and third processes, the provider identifies its internal strengths and weaknesses as a provider of workplace language training and analyzes external factors to identify the opportunities and threats that are present in the business environment. These two steps are often referred to as the SWOT (strengths, weaknesses, opportunities, threats) analysis. The fourth process involves setting goals and creating marketing and development strategies that will allow the provider to build on its strengths, address its weaknesses, capitalize on opportunities, and manage threats.

The knowledge and perspective gained from each of these processes informs the others. All four take place simultaneously, and no single one is complete until all are.

Effective workplace language training providers typically engage in four concurrent practices as part of the strategic planning process.

Practice 1.1: articulate mission and values

Practice 1.2: identify internal strengths and weaknesses

Practice 1.3: analyze external opportunities and threats

Practice 1.4: set goals and create development and marketing strategies

▦ Practice 1.1: Articulate Mission and Values

An effective workplace language training provider has thought through its purpose and objectives and distilled that thinking into a working mission statement that makes clear what it provides, for whom, how, where, and why. The provider refines and refocuses the mission statement during its SWOT analysis.

What

The *what* statement answers the questions, What does the provider do? and What is its function? For effective workplace language training providers, the function is to provide the type of English language instruction known in the profession as English for occupational purposes (EOP), English for business purposes (EBP), or English for professional purposes (EPP). The *what* statement thus reflects the fact that workplace English language training is central to the provider's identity, not a sideline or accidental activity, and that resources and attention are dedicated accordingly.

Who

The *who* statement addresses target clients and target populations. A workplace language training provider may choose to limit the types of corporate, government, or nonprofit clients with whom it works. A provider may also specify the populations for which it provides training: recent immigrants seeking to enter the workforce, hourly wage employees, managers, and executives. An effective workplace language training provider makes conscious decisions about its specialization and its market niche on the basis of its size, expertise, values, and market environment.

How

The *how* statement describes the way(s) in which the workplace language training provider fulfills its function. *How* includes the types of services, programs, and educational products that the provider makes available as well as whether its programs are original or customized versions of existing programs. *How* also includes the types and levels of technology that the provider employs and the amount of time and energy that it devotes to research and development. Finally, *how* may include a statement of the way in which a provider attracts its clients: through reliability, quality, or cost savings. An effective workplace language training provider takes a focused, rather than a haphazard, approach to defining these techniques and methods.

Where

The *where* statement addresses two aspects of location: the geographic area(s) in which the provider operates and the physical location in which training takes place. On-site training takes place in the client's facilities; off-site training, though generally not highly recommended, takes place in provider facilities or in another location. A provider that conducts distance learning or Web-based training may also include a statement about the location(s) from which access is available. An effective workplace language training provider has thought through location options and selected those that fit its capabilities to best serve client needs.

Why

In the *why* statement, a provider articulates its reason for being. A *why* statement may be as broad as, "To improve the quality of communication in the workplace" or as narrow as, "To ensure the safety of airline passengers by improving pilots' command of English." An effective workplace language training provider can articulate a *why* statement that reflects its values and clarifies the answers to the other questions.

Provider Model

The answers to each of these questions will depend in large part on provider type or model, so it is useful for a provider to define its model as part of its mission statement. The following list represents various types of providers that deliver language training programs in the workplace. Some providers may represent combinations of these models.

- internal corporate provider, either a company training division or professional development center, or a part of an industry-based consortium, employer association, or employee organization
- corporate training company
- educational institution
- government-funded organization, either a domestic agency funded by local, state/provincial, or national government, or a development organization funded through government-backed international development agencies
- private consultant or private consulting group
- private or franchised language service or school
- nongovernmental organization (NGO)

A provider model may dictate the response to the *who* and *where* questions. An internal provider, for example, would serve only company employees in a location provided by the company; a government-funded organization would serve a government-mandated constituency; an educational institution might provide off-site training at its own facilities instead of or in addition to on-site programs, though the latter is preferable. A provider model may also govern the response to the *what* question. A corporate training company or a language school might provide proprietary training programs customized to client needs; a government-funded organization may be required to use standardized assessments and training materials, a less effective situation.

Values

The responses to the questions outlined above, especially the *how* and *why* questions, are also closely tied to the provider's value system. For this reason, clarification of values and priorities is an important part of the strategic planning process. Such clarification involves recognizing the relative weight of potentially opposing goals. Growth and profit often must be balanced against the need for security; the desire for conflict avoidance; and provider quality, accountability, and ethical stance.

Security
Some geographic locations and types of clients can pose financial and physical risks to a workplace language training provider. Corporate or government funding for training programs may be reduced or disappear completely due to changes in a developing nation's economic status. Terrorism or war may pose physical threats to the provider's personnel.

Taking such risks can enable a provider to develop new expertise and new client bases, and, consequently, new opportunities for growth and profit. For a nonprofit provider whose purpose is to serve populations in developing nations (e.g., an NGO), facing the risks posed by terrorism or war may be an inherent part of mission fulfillment. A provider that operates in risk-laden environments must determine at what point security considerations outweigh the potential for growth, profit, or the ability to serve its target population.

Conflict Avoidance
In identifying its target market and the services it provides, a provider needs to assess its tolerance for competition with other providers and delimit its market niche accordingly. The broader its target market, the greater the possibility for profit, but also the greater the exposure to competition. A provider must decide at what point the costs in time and resources of dealing with competition become greater than the potential benefits. It can also consider, however, the potential benefits of collaborating with its competition.

Quality and Accountability
One fundamental role of any workplace language training provider is to guide clients' expectations by projecting outcomes based on the time, effort, and money the client is able to invest. A provider sets its definition of program quality and determines the minimum levels of time, effort, and compensation required to ensure that quality. Reducing program time or level of effort by decreasing the needs assessment, instructional time, or program support may make a program more attractive from a cost perspective but may also compromise the quality of the program and reduce the provider's ability to be accountable (i.e., to do what it has said it will do). A provider must decide at what point unrealistic expectations or financial limitations will make projects untenable.

Ethical Stance
In selecting the types of opportunities that it will pursue, a provider needs to determine whether some types of clients or projects are unacceptable for ethical reasons. A broader client base provides greater opportunities for growth and profit but may place the provider in the position of supporting the activities of a government that abuses human rights or a corporation with questionable accounting practices. A workplace language training provider must determine whether and to what extent such activities will make a potential client or project unacceptable.

Case Study 1.1: Nonprofit Organization Develops Mission Statement

In developing its mission statement, a newly founded nonprofit organization focused initially on its *why* statement: To provide educational services that would empower residents of developing nations to participate in and contribute to their countries' growth. Its *what* statement listed the types of education with which it would begin—business fundamentals and EFL—and the types that it hoped to offer in the future. The mission statement also named the countries in which the organization intended to operate and briefly described its way of operating.

Recognizing the nature of life in developing nations, the organization gave special attention to the articulation of its values with regard to risk and ethical stance. The organization outlined broad guidelines for determining when a program was too risky to implement or to continue and when a project was unacceptable because of its potential connection with human rights violations.

This level of clarity was invaluable to the organization when it needed to sort out the complexities of working in a particular nation. Recognizing the dangers inherent in the political situation and the government's mixed record, the organization determined that the potential for positive outcomes outweighed the risks to its personnel, but that it would need to limit its offerings in order to maintain its value system. The organization agreed to develop and conduct EFL programs for human rights activists and judges from the national ministry of justice, but declined a request to teach English to police interrogators of alleged terrorists.

Practice 1.2: Identify Internal Strengths and Weaknesses

In developing its strategic plan, an effective workplace language training provider conducts an internal inventory of its structures and systems. This inventory enables it to identify the strengths and weaknesses in the way it operates and to assess the effect of these strengths and weaknesses on its ability to provide appropriate levels of responsiveness, flexibility, quality, and accountability for its clients.

Study of strengths and weaknesses also enables a provider to identify the area or areas in which it has distinctive competency or competencies—the characteristic that sets it apart from other providers. A distinctive competency may be a program specialization, such as working with middle managers who must relate to their counterparts in other countries or providing coaching to busy, high-level executives. A distinctive competency may also be an ability or knowledge base, such as expertise in a particular industry area or ability to conduct training programs in specific countries.

Information for the inventory of strengths and weaknesses can be gathered from interviews with staff members; a review of organizational literature, including annual reports, project reports, and Web site; feedback from colleagues, program participants, and client contacts; and exit interview information from former staff.

Areas to be inventoried include

- management structure: the number and extent of management levels and the relationships among different positions

- marketing and new client development: how it is handled and how it is connected with ongoing client relations

- client relations and management: how proposals are developed, presented, and modified; how contracts and fees are negotiated; how programs are managed; and how follow-up is handled

- program development: how programs are designed, how materials are developed, how program results are evaluated, and how quality control is maintained

- staff: required qualifications, including educational background and experience, how staff are evaluated, and the extent and means of professional development

- public relations: how the organization interacts with the community at large

- facilities: available space and equipment, including technology support

- operations: how accounts receivable, accounts payable, payroll, legal services, licensing and registration, and other day-to-day business matters are handled

For most workplace language training providers, analysis of strengths and weaknesses is tied to the skills and expertise of specific staff members. The smaller the organization, the greater the potential influence of individual knowledge and abilities. Effective workplace language training providers use outside facilitators or other neutral parties and mechanisms to help them analyze strengths and weaknesses in ways that are impartial, nonjudgmental, and supportive.

Practice 1.3: Analyze External Opportunities and Threats

Following an internal analysis of strengths and weaknesses, a provider turns to evaluation of the opportunities and threats present in its current and potential operating environment. To do this, the provider begins by identifying the industry sectors, geographic areas, and workforce populations in which a need for workplace EOP is evident. The provider then analyzes circumstances and trends in each area to identify the opportunities for growth and threats to success that a given area poses.

An analysis of opportunities for workplace language training can be facilitated by the use of traditionally recognized categories of industry: the extractive category, which makes use of resources from the land or water; the manufacturing category; the service category; the government-civilian category; the government-military category; and the NGO category. The United States and many other countries have standardized ways of categorizing industries that can help a provider understand how industry sectors are related to one another and how information about them is presented in government and other sources. The older U.S. system of standardized industrial classification (SIC) codes and descriptions (U.S. Department of Labor, 1987; http://www.osha.gov/oshstats/sicser.html) is being replaced by the North American Industry Classification System (NAICS; U.S. Census Bureau, 1997; http://www.census.gov/pub/epcd/www.naics.html) and North American Product Classification System (NAPCS), joint projects of the United States, Canada, and Mexico designed to make business information and statistics comparable across the three nations.

The European Community uses the NACE system (nomenclature générale des activités économiques dan les communautés Européennes, or general industrial classification of economic activites within the European communities). Japan uses the Japanese Standard Industrial

Case Study 1.2: Consulting Group Reconsiders Strengths and Weaknesses

A consulting group used the occasion of its fifth anniversary to revisit its mission statement and revise its strategic plan. The group had been founded by four consultants, each of whom had background in a different area of industry. For the first 5 years of its existence, the group had focused on providing services to corporate clients in those four areas, with each consultant handling a specific type of client from contact to proposal to program to evaluation. This initial strategy had enabled the group to establish a firm client base and to develop a reputation as a responsive provider of quality language training programs.

With the guidance of a facilitator, the consultants explored the strengths and weaknesses of the group and discovered that what had originally been a strength had become in some ways a liability. Opportunities with the federal government and corporations in industry areas beyond the original four had expanded the client base to the point where the single-contact approach was no longer feasible. It had become physically impossible for the consultants as individuals to handle all aspects of the client relationship for the number of clients they were now serving.

The consultants examined two traits that they felt had formed the basis for their success: their knowledge of four specific industry areas and the fact that each client had the same point of contact throughout the client-provider relationship. Comments on client evaluations had shown that their clients valued the security of having a knowledgeable consultant and the ease with which they were able to call the same contact person.

To continue growing, the consultants needed to find a more efficient way to manage programs. To maintain their quality reputation, they needed to continue providing the level of comfort to which their clients had become accustomed. Through facilitated discussion, the consultants determined that they could strike a balance by hiring a program manager to handle the logistics of program setup, maintenance, and evaluation. This would free the consultants themselves to focus on client and program development. By introducing the program manager personally to all existing clients, making frequent check-in phone calls to their clients when programs were in progress, and assuring clients that they would be available to talk at need, the consultants would maintain the quality relationships that their clients so prized.

Classification, or JSIC. Further, many countries directly use, or correlate their own systems to, the United Nations (UN) system: the International Standard Industrial Classification System (ISICS).

A second useful distinction can be made among types of workforce populations: executives, management, skilled labor, and unskilled labor. A workplace language training provider can control the analytical process by investigating one geographic area, industry category, or workforce segment at a time.

A provider uses the general and specialized news media, online sources, government data, and industry contacts to obtain the information it needs for its analysis of opportunities and threats. The governments of many countries have services that conduct labor market research and make the results available in print and on the World Wide Web. For example, in the United States, the Bureau of Labor Statistics of the U.S. Department of Labor (2002) provides a *Career Guide to Industries* (http://www.bls.gov/oco/cg/home.htm) that contains much potentially useful information about various industry sectors, as does the site of the Labor Department's America's Labor Market Information System (ALMIS; n.d.; http://www.doleta.gov/almis). Labor market information for individual states is available on state Web sites.

Private online sources also provide detailed information about the current status and prospects of industry sectors and individual companies throughout the world. The Riley Guide has a section that refers users to online business research collections (Dikel, 2002; http://www.rileyguide.com/employer.html#industry). Many corporate annual reports are available from the *Wall Street Journal*'s (n.d.) online service (http://wsjie.ar.wilink.com/cgi-bin/start.pl), and Hoover's Directory of Companies provides online information on specific companies as well as industry sectors (http://www.hoovers.com; this site charges a fee for service).

In addition, the extensive, printed annual directories published by Moody's Industrial Manuals, provides comprehensive data on corporations that trade on the New York Stock Exchange and the American Exchange.

Once the provider determines in which industry sectors, workforce segments, and geographic areas a need for workplace language training is evident, and whether that need is increasing (opportunity) or decreasing (threat), it can consider other factors that may affect its potential operations.

Economic Factors

Answering a few questions about the characteristics of and trends in a country's economy enables a provider to recognize opportunities for and threats to operations. As a U.S. Department of Education-designated national resource center for international business, the Eli Broad Graduate School of Management at Michigan State University (2002) maintains an information Web site that provides detailed information about the business and economic climate in countries throughout the world (http://globaledge.msu.edu/ibrd/ibrd.asp). A provider needs to determine

- whether the country is considered developed or developing, from an economic perspective

- whether it is a state-run economy, a market economy, or an economy in transition

- how companies in an emerging-market economy are supposed to be handling contracts and payments, and how they actually handle them

- which industry sectors are large and which are small, in terms of size and revenue

- which industry sectors are strong and expanding, and which are weak and shrinking

- how globally or domestically oriented various industry sectors are, how diverse their workforces are, and to what extent various industries target domestic and foreign markets

This review of economic factors allows a workplace language training provider to identify which industry sectors are viewed as priorities for a given country and may be targeted for language training. The review also permits a provider to anticipate problems that may arise from breach-of-contract or nonpayment situations. Finally, the review can help a provider define its own potential role if it sees itself as an active participant in language planning and language policy efforts on behalf of the adult labor force in its geographic market.

Political Factors

Political factors can affect the environment for workplace language training in crucial ways. They may precipitate the opening of a previously closed society. Conversely, political factors such as an international embargo or military conflict may close down a market. Factors to consider include the type and stability of the government and the regional alliance of which it is or seeks to be a member of. In terms of politics and language, the workplace language training provider also considers official language(s), language of business and government, and existing or pending language-related legislation. Finally, at a microlevel, the workplace language training provider considers whether government censorship policies have any direct impact on the content of language training materials.

Technology and Related Infrastructure Factors

Technological and infrastructure factors may limit or expand the ability of a workplace language training provider to function in a given geographic location. These factors include the reliability of the supply of electricity, the reliability and availability of wire-based or wireless communication technologies, and the availability and affordability of computer equipment and Internet access. A workplace language training provider also considers the usual level of technology in educational and training environments (e.g., blackboard and chalk, overhead projectors, computers) and customary modes of delivery (e.g., classroom instruction, distance learning, tutoring).

Legal Factors

A workplace language training provider must be aware of a variety of legal factors that can affect its operations in a given country. These include

- laws governing the employment of foreign workers and local workers by a foreign entity
- requirements for certification, licensing, and insurance
- laws governing contracting

Country-by-country information on the laws and business customs surrounding international trade is available in print publications, such as Dun & Bradstreet's (1996) *Exporter's Encyclopedia*.

Social Factors

A workplace language training provider must be aware of social factors and societal conventions that may affect its operations. Instruction of one gender by the other or of members of one religious, ethnic, or social group by a member of another may be banned by societal norms, even when not prohibited by law.

Competition

A major external factor is the provider's competition, or the other providers operating in its market. Competition can come from companies' internal training divisions as well as from other independent providers. A provider needs to look at trends in training to assess whether outsourcing is on the rise and internal training is decreasing or vice versa.

To the extent possible, a provider also needs to gather the same information about the strengths and weaknesses of other providers that it gathered about itself, but it needs to look at this information in terms of the opportunities and threats that other providers pose in the marketplace. The strength of the pre-existing competition can be a major barrier to entry into a given market, especially for a small firm with a limited budget for advertising and marketing. On the other hand, competitor analysis can lead to finding a collaborator, or opportunity, as well as to identifying a competitor, or threat.

Client Expectations

Finally, a provider must consider the expectations for training design, training outcomes, and costs that exist in the marketplace. Previously established norms that are difficult for a provider to match constitute a major barrier to entry. On the other hand, a provider that can exceed expectations in one or more ways has a real competitive advantage.

Having conducted a thorough analysis of opportunities and threats, an effective workplace language training provider uses the information it has gained to guide its activities. Especially in EFL settings, where clients often approach providers on their own initiative, effective providers use their analysis to keep such opportunities in perspective, rather than being pulled in multiple, spontaneous directions with the appearance of every caller at the door. Such use of its own analysis of opportunities and threats allows a provider to stay focused on and in control of its business in order to be fully responsive to all of its clients.

Case Study 1.3: Franchised Language Schools in Egypt Reconsider Opportunities and Threats

A chain of franchised language schools in Egypt provided English language instruction, Arabic for foreigners, secretarial studies, and English teacher training. The chain of four schools—with nearly 100 teachers and 5,500 students—was a successful, ongoing operation. The chain's owner recognized that he had had a near monopoly on the market for almost 10 years. This was because he had been the first (and only) person to establish a quality, private language school in Egypt after President Anwar Sadat opened the country to the West and to private enterprise in 1974.

In the early 1980s, a threat to this monopoly emerged as a number of new private language schools began to compete with the franchise. In analyzing this competition, the owner recognized that, with their air conditioning and fine furnishings, the new schools were targeting the high-end clientele that he served through his English department and Arabic for foreigners department. He determined that it would be difficult to match the low prices that the new schools were offering and still continue to offer the quality instruction that was one of the franchise's distinguishing features.

Rather than try to expand his high-end clientele, the owner elected to continue his offerings to this population at existing costs while seeking other opportunities for growth. He observed that the market for workplace English (or English for occupational purposes [EOP]) was largely untapped and decided to move in that direction, hiring a specialist to set up the new department. This opportunity allowed him to build on an existing strength—the knowledge of the workplace that his staff had gained through the secretarial studies program and through working with the professional population that had participated in English and Arabic language training.

True to the owner's expectations, the department worked well. He had been prepared to run it at a loss for up to 2 years while it was getting established, but it actually broke even in both of its first 2 years.

Practice 1.4: Set Goals and Create Development and Marketing Strategies

Once a provider has developed its mission statement, outlined its values, and identified its internal strengths and weaknesses and the external opportunities and threats that it faces, it can synthesize this information into a set of goals supported by development and marketing strategies.

The workplace language training provider should identify the opportunities that it believes best match its strengths and distinctive competencies, and develops its goals from these. A provider's goals may be program oriented: to increase the percentage of participants who complete training or to refine program offerings to better match client needs. Goals may also be market oriented: to increase the provider's client base within a particular industry sector, to broaden its reach to specific new industry sectors, or to develop longer term relationships and repeat business with existing clients. Whatever the goals and however many there are, an essential feature of goal formulation is identification of the provider's strength or distinctive competency that makes each goal viable.

For each goal it outlines, the provider needs to develop clear definitions of success and failure. These may be defined in whatever terms are relevant to the provider: number of clients, rate of increase of client base, visibility and reputation, number of program participants, increase in participants' English language proficiency, or profit level. To make sense for the provider, however, the definitions need to be consonant with the provider's mission and value system.

Effective workplace language training providers have explicit definitions of success and failure that help them determine when a goal has been met or is no longer viable. This proactive approach ensures that the provider controls its situation and is able to move ahead with successful initiatives while minimizing losses from unsuccessful ones.

Finally, for each goal it outlines, the provider needs to address internal weaknesses and external threats that may affect its ability to take full advantage of the opportunity, outlining the development strategy it will use to address the areas of weakness and the marketing strategy it will use to pursue the opportunity while managing threats.

Development Strategy

A development strategy gives the specifics of how a provider will address weaknesses that may affect its ability to accomplish a goal. The strategy consists of a gap analysis, an approach, and a series of action steps keyed to a time line.

The gap analysis shows why the weakness is a weakness by defining the difference between where the provider currently is and where it needs to be to accomplish its goal. Much of the gap analysis takes place while the provider is analyzing strengths and weaknesses and aids the provider in determining realistically which gaps it can or should close.

The provider then identifies the approach or approaches it will use to close the gap. The approach may involve changing the way operations are managed, changing the management structure, hiring additional staff with desired areas of expertise, training existing staff to broaden or deepen their skills, or acquiring different or additional physical facilities.

Having identified its approach, the provider outlines the action steps it will take and sequences them on a time line. As it does this, the provider assesses what each step will cost in terms of time, money, and other resources.

This process enables the provider to double-check the feasibility of its development strategy. Successful development strategies are clearly connected with the strategies they are intended to support and enhance the provider's ability to accomplish its mission. Their action steps and time lines offer the provider a clear, though possibly challenging, path to follow. This gives the provider a feeling of accountability to itself that spurs implementation of the plan.

Marketing Strategy

The marketing strategy outlines the ways in which a provider intends to match its strengths to the opportunities it sees while managing the threats that may arise. In its marketing strategy, a provider describes its approach(es) and lays out a series of action steps keyed to a time line. Carrying out this detailed process enables a provider to double-check the feasibility and practicality of its plans.

Strategic marketing approaches may include redefining the provider's market niche; offering add-on services such as mentor and tutor training, study materials, and Internet-based instructional support; developing partnership or subcontractor relationships with other organizations; and using some or all of the marketing techniques described in the next section of this book.

In selecting a marketing approach, the workplace language training provider also describes the effect(s) that cultural and economic context may have on development and implementation of a marketing strategy. Effective workplace language training providers recognize which marketing techniques are acceptable and which are inappropriate or simply ineffective in the environments in which they operate, and design their marketing strategies accordingly. This point is discussed in more detail in the next section of this book.

Case Study 1.4: Small, Private School Establishes Development Goal and Marketing Strategy

Six years after its founding, a small, private school in the Washington, DC, area had established itself as a provider of English language training for foreign professionals brought to the United States by large corporations as part of their exchange programs. Recognizing that they had reached all of the corporations in that market niche, the school's president and senior staff began to seek opportunities for growth in other areas.

Talking with colleagues in the training business and with acquaintances who worked for the federal government, the school's president learned that many federal agencies were hiring increasing numbers of nonnative speakers of English to fill management and professional positions. Furthermore, changes in the approach to staff development meant that many agencies were seeking outside contractors to provide training for their employees, rather than conducting it in-house. These agencies needed a variety of training programs, including those targeting interpersonal, presentation, time management, and conflict management skills as well as ESL and intercultural communication.

Considering this opportunity, the school's president and senior staff decided that pursuing it directly was neither feasible nor desirable. None of them had experience with responding to federal requests for proposal (RFPs). More significantly, their mission centered on the provision

continued on page 13

---

continued from page 12

of English language training for nonnative speakers, and trying to develop program offerings in other content areas would require them either to develop new expertise themselves or to hire others to provide it. The latter option was not feasible for financial reasons; the former was untenable because it would likely result in a superficial knowledge that would not support the school's standards of instructional quality.

However, the continuing growth of the population of nonnative speakers in the federal workforce made the school staff reluctant to bypass the opportunity entirely. They decided, therefore, to adopt an indirect strategy that would develop their strengths over the long run while using the strengths of others in the short term.

Goal: to develop and provide on-site instructional programs in English as a second language and intercultural communication to federal employees

Strengths and distinctive competencies to build on: experience in development and provision of workplace ESL instruction, which includes an intercultural communication component

Weaknesses to address: intercultural communication does not exist as a stand-alone program; intercultural communication components of existing programs are geared only toward foreigners dealing with U.S. natives, not vice versa; no knowledge of the federal procurement and contracting system

Development strategy:

Approach = Develop existing programs and staff

Action plan and time line = Over 3 months, president will participate in federal proposal writing and contracting workshop offered by the Small Business Administration; two senior staff will participate in a train-the-trainer session in cross-cultural communication offered by the local chapter of an association for human resources professionals and develop a stand-alone intercultural communication seminar

Marketing strategy:

Approach = Market school as potential subcontractor to larger organizations that bid on federal RFPs for training services

Action plan and time line = Months 1, 2: Develop prospect list and targeted marketing materials; Month 3: Send marketing mailing to federal contractors and follow up with phone calls

Success and failure: This initiative will be a success if, after 12 months, three companies have expressed active interest in working with us as a subcontractor and one has submitted a proposal that includes our name. After the first 12 months, the initiative will be successful if it produces a sense of professional and personal satisfaction in involved staff members and generates sufficient income to cover its costs, plus 15%

The focused nature of the school's strategy, the professional attitude of its staff, and the quality of its program offerings and reputation made it an attractive partner for several area training providers. Within 12 months, the school was named as subcontractor in two submitted proposals, both eventually successful. After 3 years, federal agencies had become a significant segment of the school's client base, and school staff had gained sufficient experience in the federal procurement process to be able to respond directly to RFPs for the services they could provide.

Conclusion

The intentional process outlined in this chapter is the foundation that underlies an organization's ability to provide workplace language training programs and services that can be characterized as effective practices. The process of developing a strategic plan is a critical component of a provider's business plan. Once a workplace language training provider has built an identity for itself through articulation of its mission and values and through analysis of the internal and external factors that will contribute to or impede its success, it is ready to present itself to potential clients. This self-presentation takes place through marketing activities, as described in Effective Practice 2.

Effective Practice 2

The Workplace Language Training Provider Conducts Effective Marketing Activities

Overview

Successful marketing of workplace English language training depends on generating interest among potential clients. To do this, a workplace language training provider develops a thorough understanding of its target market and uses that understanding to create its marketing and public relations strategy. The strategy includes educating the target market about the positive outcomes of workplace language training, developing marketing materials that depict the provider and its programs and services fairly and favorably, and maintaining a positive public image. Effective providers have focused marketing and public relations strategies that result in client bases appropriate to their strengths and skills. Four practices are involved in successful marketing.

Practice 2.1: understand the target market

Practice 2.2: educate the target market

Practice 2.3: develop effective, appropriate marketing materials and techniques

Practice 2.4: maintain a positive public image

Practice 2.1: Understand the Target Market

Understanding the target market begins with identifying employers who have hired, or potentially would hire, a workforce with target-language limitations and determining their reasons for doing so. Hotels and restaurants in the United States, for example, may hire service workers who are nonnative speakers of English because of a shortage of native-born unskilled labor or an unwillingness to take such jobs. Electronics and information technology companies may hire the best qualified engineers and computer scientists, including some who are nonnative English speakers. Construction firms may employ skilled laborers whose first language is other than English in trades that are no longer widely practiced in the United States.

An international corporation, whether based in the United States or in another country, may hire staff at various levels in the geographic areas in which it operates. In such cases, fluency in English for business purposes, though desirable, is usually secondary to other job-related qualifications.

This study of potential clients' workforces goes hand in hand with understanding the businesses in which potential clients are involved. A workplace language training provider that understands what a company does and how it does it is able to discern potential benefits of English language training that the client itself has not perceived and use those in its marketing strategy.

Understanding the target market also involves recognizing the factors that determine potential clients' approach to employee training in general and to English language training in particular. Factors that affect the general approach to training may include cost, return on investment, and level of interest in providing employee advancement opportunities. The approach to English language training may be affected by customer relations, safety and efficiency considerations, employee time away from work, and awareness of the availability of training services. A major factor affecting employers' attitudes toward English language training for unskilled labor is the high turnover rate in this population. In the United States, some employers regard English language training for low-level employees as impractical: They believe that employees will not stay with the company, and the company accrues no return on its training investment. In fact, the opposite is true. Because the employees recognize the benefit of the English training program, they stay as long as the company offers it.

Effective language training providers use formal and informal networks of business colleagues, as well as their own reading and observations, to gain the information they need about the target market and specific potential clients and to keep current on trends in workforce populations. Such networking helps them know where the need for language training is increasing, where it is decreasing, and why. It ensures a thorough knowledge base that allows them to direct their marketing efforts in effective ways toward clients who are most likely to respond.

▓ Practice 2.2: Educate the Target Market

An essential task in marketing is simply to educate potential clients about the field of workplace language training. The goals of such education are to raise awareness of the need for and benefits of workplace language training, to identify workplace language training as a distinct field within the English language teaching profession, to demonstrate the advantages of language training programs that are customized to the workplace, and to define the characteristics that distinguish a high-quality language training provider.

Target market education demonstrates to potential clients that they have a need for workplace language training and illustrates the benefits that such training can provide. An organization may have been tolerating less than optimal results in customer relations, sales, daily operations and management, or employee safety, or it may be missing opportunities for change and growth because of workers' language limitations. Target market education demonstrates the ways in which workplace language training meets this need.

Effective target market education outlines what workplace language trainers do and why they do it, and then describes the outcomes that such training makes possible. One compelling

*Case Study 2.1: Consulting Group Tailors Program Brochure
to Meet Needs of Defense Contractors*

A small defense contractor based in Annapolis, Maryland, in the United States, had three employees of Asian background on its engineering staff. Highly qualified technically, these professionals made strong contributions in research and development, but lacked the English skills necessary to write effective government proposals. The contractor compensated by relying on its native speakers of English to do most of the writing and to edit the material produced by the three Asians. The company also encouraged the three engineers to enroll in a community-based ESL program.

A language training consulting group, studying the recent influx of foreign-born engineering professionals to the area, noted that many of them had found employment with defense contractors. Using its network of contacts, the consulting group learned that many smaller contractors, the Annapolis company among them, did not have internal training divisions and were reluctant to invest training dollars in a consultant-provided program that met such a limited need.

The consulting group considered sending general marketing material to the Annapolis firm and others like it, but rejected this approach. Studying the defense contracting industry further, the group learned that, in order to compete successfully in a tight market, smaller defense contractors needed to maintain a high profile in the technical community. This involved having upper level staff members publish technical papers and research reports in trade journals and other professional venues.

The consulting group realized that one member's background in technical writing would allow it to develop a creative marketing strategy for the Annapolis firm and others like it. The group produced a brochure that offered a project-based program in technical writing for nonnative speakers of English. During the course of the program, participants would review written language skills, study and practice formats for proposals and reports, and produce a short technical paper that could be submitted for publication.

This marketing brochure was distributed to the heads of 50 small to medium-sized defense contracting firms. More than half called in response, and several, including the Annapolis firm, became clients of the consulting group.

technique is the use of real-life stories that include an actual cost-benefit analysis and real numbers that indicate the organization's return on its training investment. Such graphic illustrations help potential clients recognize ways in which they could benefit from workplace language training.

Education of the target market takes place through a variety of venues. Print articles may be submitted to trade journals of specific industries and publications of industry associations. Articles can also be submitted to business journals, the business section of newspapers, and publications read by human resources managers.

Radio and television interviews, in which a workplace language training provider's president or senior staff answer questions about the need for workplace language training, trends in workplace language training, and so on, can be powerful attention-getters. Interviews can subsequently be re-aired or published, increasing the potential exposure.

Meetings of industry professional societies and associations can provide opportunities for making targeted educational presentations as well as for networking and informal education through conversation. Similar opportunities may be presented by chambers of commerce and better business bureaus.

An individual workplace language training provider or a group of providers and corporate representatives can organize breakfast forums, lunch seminars, and other educational and networking opportunities for business leaders. Such initiatives can help establish the specialty of workplace language training in the perception of local business communities by increasing the visibility of and highlighting the expertise of providers.

Target market education benefits the entire workplace language training community by raising the profile of the field as a whole. An individual provider benefits from participation in market education activities such as those described here as publication and presentation opportunities make it more visible and enhance its professional reputation in the business community.

Evidence of the success of target market education is not always direct, and it may not be apparent for some time. Effective workplace language training providers treat target market education as an ongoing part of doing business. They continually seek out new opportunities and venues for communicating with the business community, recognizing that the benefits of this activity, though not immediately compensated, will ultimately have a positive effect on the bottom line.

▤ Practice 2.3: Develop Effective, Appropriate Marketing Materials and Techniques

Marketing techniques and materials are the mechanisms through which a provider builds relationships with its clients. Their purpose is to present a provider in a positive light and distinguish it from its competitors, while describing the provider's services in terms of how well suited they are to meet a client's needs. Whereas target market education aims to make a client think, "I need workplace language training," marketing materials and techniques aim to make the client think, "I need this workplace language training provider."

An important aspect of marketing is being able to discern and address a potential client's areas of constraint or resistance, such as time, cost, and management support. Effective marketing materials and techniques demonstrate a provider's awareness of such constraints and willingness to work with a client to address them.

Materials

A provider's marketing materials convey information about the provider's identity by their content and appearance. Effective materials carry a message that is clear and consistent.

Print Materials
A workplace language training provider often has three types of print materials for use in different marketing contexts. Brochures, capability statements, and business cards are designed for initial contact with potential clients, whether through marketing mailings or placement at

Case Study 2.2: Language Training Provider Uses Real-Life Story to Educate Corporate Audience

The head of a U.S.-based language training company was invited to make a presentation at a corporate breakfast forum. The presenter decided to focus her remarks on the value of providing workplace language training for nonnative speakers of English in the blue-collar workforce because, in her experience, corporate executives did not always see the advantage of making such an investment.

The presenter briefly summarized the activities of a quality workplace language training provider, including detailed needs assessment, customized program design, and targeted instruction, explaining the rationale for each. She then told the story of a batteries manufacturer with whom her firm had worked.

As older workers retired and new ones were hired, the manufacturer found itself with an increasing number of immigrant workers on its assembly line; the manufacturer did not realize that these workers were nonliterate. The company also had another problem. Although production levels on the line had remained steady, production costs and fines for toxic dumping had increased dramatically in recent years.

The company brought in the presenter's workplace language training company to provide a program in workplace-specific communication for the line workers. The company hoped that workers' improved communication skills would enable them to help managers identify the cause of the increase in production costs and environmental fines.

The provider's training company began by conducting a detailed needs assessment that involved interviewing managers, line supervisors, and line workers and observing the assembly line in action. As a result of this careful observation, the training provider discovered that the participants were nonliterate and could not read signs labeled *Waste* and *Recycle*. They had been putting rejected parts indiscriminately in either bin. Thus, parts that could be recycled were thrown away; some of these parts contained toxic material that should have been disposed of properly as hazardous waste. Other parts that should have been thrown away were recycled into production; some of these parts caused defects in new products.

The net savings to the company, once employees were able to distinguish between the bin signs, was approximately $78,000 per year.

The training company head concluded her presentation with an invitation to audience members to consider how language training might benefit their companies. Over a period of several months following the breakfast forum, a number of those who had attended called her to discuss workplace language training. Every one of the callers mentioned the impression her story had made on them.

pickup points such as conferences. The effectiveness of using these marketing materials in impersonal ways must be determined by the local cultural context.

Longer descriptions of programs and services are generally used for follow up after initial contact has been made. Newsletters give a provider a way to introduce new program offerings to existing clients and are often an important part of maintaining client relationships.

Videotape

The visual images presented in marketing videos can have high impact and marketing value. When a personal interview is not possible, a video allows a provider to reinforce the message conveyed in print materials. Effective videos are no more than 5–10 minutes long.

Web Site

Web sites have become a standard tool of marketing in developed countries, often providing a potential client its first contact with a workplace language training provider. Effective sites have a look and message that is consistent with the look and message conveyed by the provider's print material and are updated regularly to encourage repeat visits.

Techniques

Cultural factors play an important role in defining which marketing techniques are appropriate in a given country. For example, in many countries, particular customs have evolved around the giving and receiving of business cards. An effective marketing strategy employs techniques that fit the context.

Direct Marketing

A provider's ability to target likely prospects through direct marketing is built on its analysis of opportunities in various market segments and its subsequent identification, through networking, research, or inquiries, of the appropriate person to contact in each potential client company. An effective direct marketing campaign must be sensitive to cultural definitions of accepted and expected methods of initiating contact: an unsolicited telephone call or visit (cold call), a mailing with telephone follow-up, a call to request and schedule a meeting, or an introduction (personal or written) by a mutual acquaintance. Generally, the more personal the method, the more effective it is.

Effective workplace language training providers recognize the power of first impressions and use the initial contact with a potential client to lay the groundwork for a long-term relationship. They focus on gathering information about the client and the client's needs in order to be able to present comprehensive training solutions.

Display Advertising

Advertising in business and professional publications that are read by executives and senior managers raises a provider's visibility in the business community. Some workplace language trainers have gained business by putting up display ads in public places where there is much traffic in their targeted markets, such as airport terminals and local libraries.

Conference and Trade Show Exhibits

Industry association conferences and trade shows provide opportunities for workplace language training providers to increase their visibility and broaden their circle of contacts. In such venues, video clips and interactive computer demonstrations can attract attention and convey essential information quickly.

Case Study 2.3: Workplace Language Provider's Brochure
Uses Before-and-After Display to Highlight Program Value

A workplace language training firm in a midwestern city in the United States used its experience with a particular client to create an effective marketing brochure. The provider had designed and conducted a technical writing program for Chinese-speaking environmental planners at the state transportation department. Using information from this program, the provider designed a before-and-after brochure to illustrate the value of its program.

Before participating in the program, one employee took 10 hours to write an acceptable technical report, and his supervisor spent 5 hours editing and revising the text with him. The department was losing $3,390 every 20 weeks because of the extra time required for this employee to write acceptable technical reports.

After completing the writing program, the employee's writing ability was markedly improved, task time was reduced, and the department's loss was reduced to $1,350 every 20 weeks. A graphic in the brochure illustrated the savings:

$3,390	Costs sustained for 20 weeks before writing program
-$1,560	Costs still sustained after 20 weeks of writing program
$1,830	Savings realized due to writing program
-$ 700	Cost of writing program for 20 weeks for one participant
$1,130	Net savings after 20 weeks of writing course

(Lomperis, 1999; see also Martin & Lomperis, 2002)

By demonstrating the monetary savings realized by an actual client, this marketing brochure accomplished the goal of educating the target market—"I need workplace language training"— and marketing—"I need this workplace language training provider." The brochure became even more powerful when the provider, in conversation with potential clients, multiplied the figures given for one participant by the number of employees for whom the potential client needed training.

▦ Practice 2.4: Maintain a Positive Public Image

Public relations (PR) refers to the provider's control of the way it is perceived by the general public. A provider may use published material, such as brochures and press releases, interviews on radio and television, and public speaking opportunities to convey an image of itself as a good corporate citizen that makes a positive contribution to the well-being of the entire community. A positive public image can be a marketing asset, so attention to PR is a crucial part of a provider's business development activities. An effective approach to PR involves paying special attention to the types of communication that are possible and the kind of image that is appropriate in the country or area where a training provider furnishes its services.

Public image is based on public action. Participation in community support activities through advocacy, financial contributions, or employee volunteerism is a pivotal part of good PR.

Effective workplace language training providers recognize that the well-being of the community is vital to their own success. Their positive public image results from their active participation in community affairs and the contributions they make to the quality of life of all citizens.

*Case Study 2.4: Language Training Company
Deploys Public Relations Strategy to Good Purpose*

When fiscal problems forced a city government to make budget cuts, funding for the public library system was drastically reduced. The cuts meant that local branch libraries would curtail their hours of operation and reduce the size of their staffs.

Staff at a corporate training company learned of the problem when participants in a program they were conducting for a corporate client began to express concern. Many of these employees were neighbors, and they and their children relied on their local branch library for books, study space, and educational programs. Reductions in library hours and staff would deprive them of a valued resource.

The language training company saw this as a public relations opportunity. The training company contacted the branch and learned that a Friends of the Library group was forming to raise funds and awareness for the branch. The group was planning to hold a benefit book drive and sale. The provider agreed to collect and donate books itself, and to publicize the need to its clients. As a result, the corporation whose employees had first raised the issue and two other businesses collected books and made cash contributions, and volunteers from each business participated in the book sale event.

The businesses' support of the library garnered a small amount of positive media coverage and a large amount of goodwill in the neighborhood. Joint participation also strengthened the relationship between the training provider and its clients; as they worked together setting out books for the sale, the human resources director of one of the corporations said to the president of the training company, "It's good to know you care so much about our employees."

Conclusion

For effective workplace language training providers, marketing to new and existing clients is an ongoing process that keeps them in touch with changes and trends in the workplace as it keeps the provider's name and services visible in the business community. The desired outcome of marketing is that an educated and interested client will want to meet with the provider to intentionally explore ways in which workplace language training can address its communication needs. This topic is taken up in Effective Practice 3.

Effective Practice 3

The Workplace Language Training Provider Builds a Strong Client Relationship in Conducting an Organizational Needs Assessment and Developing a Proposed Program and Contract

Overview

When marketing results in an expression of interest from a potential client, the workplace language training provider moves to an individualized marketing mode, the objective of which is to build a mutually supportive relationship. Through telephone and face-to-face contact, the provider assesses the organization's needs, goals, and expectations and presents options for addressing them. In this process, the provider builds on the client education process that forms a part of its marketing strategy. The provider presents a realistic picture of what language training can and cannot accomplish and the time and effort required to achieve specific outcomes.

Building on this foundation, the provider and the client outline goals and desired outcomes for workplace language training. The provider then develops a program design that includes instructional needs assessment, instruction, assessment of participant progress, and program evaluation and presents these in a formal proposal. The proposal also specifies how client-provider communication will be maintained during the program's duration, scheduling considerations, and costs. This proposal, once agreed upon, becomes the basis for the contract.

Because negotiating (and perhaps renegotiating) a contract takes time, the provider alerts the client to the benefits of flexibility and makes sure that sufficient time is allowed for due diligence.

Throughout the interaction with the client, the workplace language training provider demonstrates that it is attentive, responsive, flexible, and accountable. This enables the client and the provider to build a relationship founded on mutual respect and trust. This approach to client relations involves five practices.

Practice 3.1: establish a relationship of mutual respect and trust

Practice 3.2: determine client needs, expectations, and goals

Practice 3.3: design a program

Practice 3.4: prepare and submit a proposal

Practice 3.5: negotiate the contract

Practice 3.1: Establish a Relationship of Mutual Respect and Trust

Successful provision of workplace language training depends on the development of a relationship in which the provider and client are mutually supportive. Such a relationship is centered on understanding and acknowledgment of one another's priorities, needs, and goals. Effective workplace language training providers lay the groundwork for development of a strong client relationship by focusing on a service delivery, rather than an academic, model. In an academic model, the provider would represent itself as the owner of knowledge and the one to set standards and parameters for training, and the client would be expected to conform to the provider's expectations. In a service delivery model, by contrast, the provider and the client are equal partners in setting expectations for the training program. Rather than acting as the sole authority figure, the provider represents itself as attentive, responsive, flexible, and accountable.

Attentiveness

A provider's first task in developing a client relationship is to listen to the client's own description of itself and its needs. By demonstrating its willingness to listen and its desire to understand, a provider conveys an attitude of respect for the client and shows that it will work with the client as a partner.

Listening enables a provider to understand the client's perception of employees' training needs and to identify logistical needs for scheduling, cost containment, and other considerations. Listening also gives a provider a sense of the culture of the company with respect to training—for example, if training is encouraged through release time, increased potential for promotion, and other positive reinforcement, or not. This gives the provider crucial information on which to base its presentation to the client and its training design.

Through careful listening, a provider gains knowledge not only of a client's training goals but also of larger corporate goals that may be affected by the provision and success of workplace language training. This knowledge allows the provider to discern ways that it can be of service to the client beyond the immediate situation that led to the client's expression of interest.

Responsiveness and Flexibility

The insights gained through listening prepare the provider to discuss the ways in which its programs and services can address the client's needs and help it achieve its goals.

For some clients or client representatives, the primary need may be to understand the potential benefits of workplace language training and of customized training programs. An effective workplace language training provider responds to this need by providing pertinent examples of increases in efficiency, productivity, worker retention, safety, and customer relations quality that have resulted from workplace language training.

In describing its programs and services, the provider outlines the ways in which it will respond to the client's needs with respect to scheduling, cost, and learning outcomes while maintaining the integrity of its work. An effective workplace language training provider is able to

Case Study 3.1: Consultant Establishes Positive Relationship With Industrial Equipment Manufacturer

The human resources director of a manufacturer of industrial equipment asked a workplace language training consulting firm to visit to discuss the possibility of developing a workplace English program for company employees. At first, the human resources director described a group of employees who worked on the shop floor. These workers, who came from a variety of Eastern European and Latin American backgrounds, needed to improve their English listening and speaking skills in order to communicate effectively with their coworkers and supervisors.

The consulting firm representative asked whether the company employed any other nonnative speakers who might need language training, and the director mentioned three systems technicians who she hoped could also participate in the training. Further questioning revealed, however, that the work of these three consisted primarily of writing technical manuals and guides for company-built equipment.

When the human resources director took the consultant on a tour of the company's facilities, the consultant had an opportunity to meet several of the shop floor employees as well as the three systems technicians. The consultant realized immediately that the oral communication skills of the technicians were considerably stronger than those of the shop floor workers and that mixing the two groups could cause the shop workers to feel intimidated and resentful.

On the way back to the human resources director's office, the director introduced the consultant to the company's chief operating officer (COO). "Great!" said the COO, a native speaker of English. "When you finish teaching them English, you can teach it to the rest of us!"

Back at the office, the consultant outlined the arguments for creating two class groups instead of one: differences in current ability, need, and employment level. The human resources director agreed with the consultant's reasoning, but stated that, even if there were more money in her ESL training budget, she would not be able to justify the expense of a second course for only three employees.

The consultant, thinking about the needs of the technicians and the COO's comment, asked if there was a need for writing instruction for systems technicians and other management-level employees. The director responded in the affirmative, noting that the COO had been complaining for months about writing skills across the board.

In its written proposal, the consulting firm outlined two separate courses: an ESL course for the shop floor workers, which would focus on oral communication skills, and a writing program for systems technicians. The latter course would include 1 hour a week of instruction, especially for the three nonnative speakers, in addition to the regular sessions.

Because the writing course was not exclusively an ESL course, the human resources director was able to fund it out of a different budget line from the oral communication course. Upon completion of the two courses, the director wrote a testimonial that read, in part, "The aspect that impressed us most was the way this consulting firm paid attention to our needs and worked with our system to create a win-win situation for everyone involved."

outline options for balancing achievement of learning goals against the need to contain costs and meet scheduling restrictions.

Accountability

An effective workplace language training provider knows the points beyond which it cannot compromise with regard to instructional content, program length and schedule, number of participants per class group, and cost. It presents an honest picture of the level of time and effort that will be required to achieve the learning outcomes that the client desires and provides information on how it will assess participants' progress and evaluate the program overall.

A provider illustrates its accountability while reinforcing its positive image by presenting testimonials from other clients and summary evaluations of other workplace language training programs it has conducted.

Provider and client build a relationship of mutual respect and trust as they outline needs, design a program, and work through the proposal and contract phases. For an effective workplace language training provider, the ultimate goal of every activity is the creation and maintenance of such a strong client relationship.

▨ Practice 3.2: Determine Client Needs, Expectations, and Goals

Needs

A workplace language training provider conducts an organizational needs assessment to gain as thorough an understanding as possible of the ways that English is used in the client's workplace. This process gives the provider the information it needs to design training programs that will meet needs the client may not have recognized as well as those it perceives.

Organizational needs assessment begins with understanding what the client organization does and how it does it. The provider meets with client representatives who can describe the organization's local, national, and international activities and the need for written and oral command of English associated with each. The provider also seeks to understand the client organization's view of itself, its services, and how it operates because this can have an impact on language needs. For example, a company that places a value on high-quality goods and services to meet the customized needs of individual clients has vastly different communication patterns from a company that places emphasis on the rapid turnover of mass-market goods and services. In addition, although all companies are interested in increasing productivity, employee concerns and language requirements differ, depending on whether a particular company tries to increase productivity by cutting expenses or by modernizing and expanding.

Client representatives can also outline the client company's organizational structure, the ways in which employees at different levels need to be able to use oral and written English for communication within and outside of the company, and the extent to which employees' current English skills are sufficient or insufficient for job performance. In many cases, the client has gained insight into these matters through oral or written customer feedback, which can be shared with the provider. Client representatives can also indicate the relationship between improved language skills and the possibility of career advancement for the employees who will participate in training.

The provider seeks to understand the communication needs and problems that exist within the organization from the client's point of view. This enables the provider to discern what the client feels it needs, whether general work-related English, task-specific language, or English as the basis for participating in technical training or obtaining a license or certificate, and to know how the client prioritizes those needs.

A workplace language training provider also seeks to learn as much as possible about the employees for whom it will be designing training, including their linguistic and cultural backgrounds, their educational levels and training experience, and any other factors that may affect their ability to participate fully in and benefit from a training program. To the degree possible at this stage, the provider augments the information gained from its primary client contacts with conversations with potential program participants, observations of employees on the job, and collection of sample work-related written material.

Employees may have language learning goals that differ from, or even oppose, those of the employer: Employers want employees to improve their English so that they can do their jobs better, whereas employees want to improve their English so that they can get better jobs. A workplace language training provider that is aware of such differences early on can address them with the client before they subvert the training program.

Finally, a workplace language training provider seeks to identify ways in which the client can create a climate that supports the ongoing development of employee language skills over the long term. One way to develop such a climate is to have the language training provider train supervisors or other employees as tutors and mentors. These people can enhance the effect of a workplace language training program by reinforcing learning while the program is taking place (especially for distance learning or computer-based training), supporting retention and further learning after it ends, and making the connection between language proficiency and the potential for promotion and career development.

Effective workplace language training providers take time to consult with as many stakeholders as possible, including potential program participants, their supervisors, and upper level management and executives. These providers recognize that inviting stakeholder involvement in the planning stages creates a level of commitment on the part of all stakeholders that is crucial to the later success of the training program.

Expectations

A workplace language training provider works most effectively with a client organization when the provider recognizes the client's expectations for training program implementation. The language that a client uses to describe its experiences with training tells the provider what the client expects in terms of training methods, training outcomes, and the level of interaction that the client will have with the provider while training is taking place. Careful listening also allows the provider to identify the sources of past success and failure in training, whether based on program design and instructional methodology or on logistical considerations, such as program length and schedule, training location, and participant attendance.

Effective workplace language training providers raise logistical considerations early in discussions with a client, recognizing that advance preparation is better than crisis management. Logistical topics for discussion include program delivery, program scheduling and location, participant recruitment, and client support.

- How will training be delivered: through traditional classroom instruction, distance learning, computer-based training, or a combination?

- Will proficiency in the use of highly technical equipment and the language relating to it be an expected training outcome? If so, would the program be strengthened by having a company employee who is a technical expert coteach part of the program with the training provider?

- If tutors or mentors are to be trained, how will their training mesh with the larger program?

- Will the program take place on company time, on employees' off time, or a combination? How will the training schedule mesh with employees' regular work schedules? Will there be a hiatus in the program during specific religious or national holidays, during heavy work times, or during employees' vacation times?

- Will the program take place on or off site? Will the same training space be available for every class session?

- Will training be mandatory? If it will be voluntary, how will participants be recruited or selected for the program? What attendance policy will be set?

- To what extent can the client provide support services, such as audio visual equipment, duplicating, and storage space for instructional materials?

- How will participation in training contribute to employees' opportunities for career advancement or readiness for changes in the workplace? How will this be communicated to them?

- In what ways can the provider coordinate its training with other programs available to employees within the client company or in the community?

The workplace language training provider recognizes the client's expectations and constraints with regard to the training schedule and avoids the trap of equating language training and learning with the imperatives of a university or language school schedule. The provider also determines what the client expects with regard to the frequency of participant progress assessments and reports and seeks to accommodate those expectations.

Finally, the workplace language training provider seeks information on how the client evaluates training programs. A client may have an in-house method that assesses general overall factors (e.g., Did participants like the trainer, the training materials, the training room?) and specific outcomes (e.g., Did training increase productivity, safety, employee retention?) An effective workplace language training provider seeks to understand a client's evaluation system and design a training program whose results can be evaluated by that system.

Goals

When the provider and the client have outlined the organization's training needs and the resources that the client is able to devote to workplace language training, they are in a position to define realistic goals for a training program. The articulation of realistic proficiency goals depends on the provider's honest appraisal of the skill development that can take place in a defined period of time. Provider and client work together to balance the need for training (more training time) against the need to contain expenses (less training time) in order to arrive at goals that are satisfactory and achievable.

Goals for workplace language training can address one or more of three broad areas:

1. language skills that will enable employees to do their current jobs effectively

2. language skills that will enable employees to manage anticipated changes or transitions in the workplace

3. language skills that will enable employees to advance in their careers

Goals may be phrased as performance objectives that state what training program participants will know and be able to do at the conclusion of the training program. For example, where employees need learn to greet customers as they enter a store, the goal could be, "Participants who complete the program will be able to use appropriate greetings for different times of day and recognize and respond to typical customer greetings." Alternatively, goals may be phrased as participant accomplishments: "Participants who complete the program will have reviewed and practiced typical greetings in class, used them on the job, and reported back to the class."

Effective workplace language training providers recognize that the goal-setting process provides an opportunity to evaluate its compatibility with a client and the potential success of the relationship. At this point, if a client has goals that the provider believes cannot be achieved, or has needs that the provider cannot address, the provider acknowledges the incompatibility and reformulates the relationship or steps away from it altogether.

Case Study 3.2: Language Training Agency in Middle East Responds to Needs of Telecommunications Company

The project manager of a telecommunications company working in a joint venture in the Middle East sent some of the local workforce (which included guest workers with a different language from another country) to an English program to improve communication on the job with English-speaking supervisors. The project manager was soon frustrated, however, by the workers' lack of progress in acquiring the English vocabulary and language skills they needed to perform on the job.

The manager communicated his frustration to the head of the language training agency that provided the English program. His staff, he said, were not learning about *pairs* as in *pair of wires* (red/green, yellow/black)—standard terminology for installing phone lines. Instead, they were learning about *pair of shoes, pair of pants, pair of scissors*.

The agency head explained that the English program was really for general English, not for the language of the workplace and of job performance, and therefore was not designed to meet the expectations and goals that the program manager had in mind. She offered to conduct a needs assessment and design a program that would meet the specific needs of the telecommunications company workers. The needs assessment would enable her to identify priority terminology in the job functions of phone line installers so that appropriate vocabulary and language structures, including the appropriate kind of *pairs*, would be included in the training provided.

Practice 3.3: Design a Program

Designing a program means outlining the overall features that will make a language training program work effectively. The design for a program includes program goals; participant recruitment, grouping, and attendance; instructional needs assessment; staffing; program logistics, such as location, schedule, and client support; progress assessment and reporting, and program evaluation. It does not include specifics of curriculum design or the design of instructional materials.

In designing a program, the workplace language training provider synthesizes its knowledge of adult pedagogy with its assessment of the client's needs and its understanding of the client's expectations to create a program that will achieve the goals that client and provider have outlined. The process of designing a program and describing that design in a written proposal is crucial for the provider. It gives the provider an opportunity to think through all aspects of the project, identify areas where its understanding or information is incomplete, and anticipate topics that will require further discussion with the client.

Program Goals

The overall program goals that the client and the provider have developed are stated at the beginning of the program design. These goals outline what participants will know and be able to do at the conclusion of the program, and so are the determinants that guide all other aspects of program design.

Participant Recruitment, Grouping, and Attendance

When training is not mandated for a specific group of employees, the client and the provider develop a strategy for recruiting participants to the program. In client organizations with established training divisions, training bulletins and fliers can be useful recruiting tools. In many cases, however, word of mouth and supervisor encouragement are the most effective mechanisms. The provider's visits to the workplace as part of the organizational needs assessment can also generate expressions of interest.

Piloting a training program can also generate significant interest while giving provider and client an opportunity to identify and address areas where the program does not meet the stated goals. Effective pilot programs are small in size and target highly motivated participants. When they have completed the training, these participants often become the program's most powerful recruiting mechanism.

The provider also helps the client to identify appropriate incentives and to recognize and reduce disincentives to participation. Client-determined incentives may include paid release time, convenience of scheduling and location, and potential for pay increases and promotion. The increased self-esteem that comes with improved language skills, itself a powerful incentive, can be reinforced through provision of a certificate for each employee who successfully completes the training program. Often, however, the reduction or removal of disincentives is the most important step a client organization can take. With training programs that take place on site and on paid release time, the most common disincentive is the conflict between completion of work assignments and attendance at the training session. When training takes place off site or on employees' own time, disincentives are often related to transportation issues, family needs, and lack of compensation. Effective workplace language training providers are sensitive to such possibilities and help clients identify and address as many as possible in the program planning stages.

The workplace language training provider also helps the client understand how participants should be grouped in order to maximize training quality and effectiveness. This often involves balancing competing needs, as the client organization may want to place as many people as possible in one group to contain costs. An effective workplace language training provider clarifies the relationship between number of participants and quality of instruction to show the client why it recommends a particular minimum or maximum class size. In this way, the provider illustrates how two smaller groups generate a better return on investment than one large group.

The provider also guides the grouping of participants. Effective providers avoid grouping managerial- and nonmanagerial-level employees together, as this creates tensions that impede learning for all participants. Beyond that, where numbers permit, providers group participants according to the work tasks that they perform rather than by language proficiency. Such a grouping enables the provider to develop a training curriculum and materials that target specific job-related communication needs for each group, increasing the effectiveness of the training program.

Finally, the provider and the client establish an attendance policy. Having identified incentives and disincentives to participation and elicited client input on its ability to provide incentives and reduce disincentives, the provider is able to outline realistic expectations for attendance and to suggest ways of addressing attendance problems if they arise.

Instructional Needs Assessment

In the program design, the workplace language training provider outlines how it will conduct a detailed instructional needs assessment. This involves assessing the ways in which employees need to use oral and written English on the job and their current ability to use it. Depending on the goals of the program with regard to oral and written use of language, instructional needs assessment may involve observation of employees on the job, one-on-one interviews, administration of a written assessment, and review of written workplace materials.

The need to conduct a careful instructional needs assessment before beginning instruction is often difficult for clients to understand. The additional time and cost may seem prohibitive. Effective workplace language training providers are able to provide anecdotal evidence to illustrate the value of a full needs assessment. They demonstrate that the assessment process allows them to develop a targeted curriculum and task-specific instructional materials that make language training more efficient in the long run. Instructional needs assessment actually increases the client's return on training investment by ensuring that training is appropriate to participants' proficiency levels and language needs.

Staffing

The provider indicates the level of staffing that will be required to run the program, including instructors and, for more extensive programs, a program manager and possibly an administrative assistant. The number of instructors needed is determined by the decisions made with regard to class size and grouping of participants.

Long-term programs that will provide training for large numbers of employees may also employ a curriculum development specialist to create curricula and materials that are linked across proficiency levels. When a client wants the provider to develop a workplace-specific assessment tool for its employees or to use standardized tests (a less effective option) to assess employees' proficiency and progress, an assessment specialist may be added to the staffing roster.

In outlining staffing, the provider also describes the role(s) that company technical specialists will play in coteaching, if technical knowledge is part of the training goal. Finally, if supervisors or other company employees are to be trained as tutors or mentors, the provider describes the roles they will play in instruction.

Program Logistics

The provider outlines the logistical considerations that will characterize the program, including schedule, location, technology, and resources support.

The determination of schedule, including class meeting times, individual class duration, and overall program duration, relies on input from client and provider. The client informs the provider about daily work schedules and seasons of the year when participation in training may prove difficult because of heavy workloads, holidays, or other conflicts. The client also indicates its preferences for training schedule, whether full time intensive (e.g., 6–8 hours/day, 5–6 days/week, for a determined number of weeks), short term, part time (e.g., 1–2 hours/session, 3–5 sessions/week, for 6–12 weeks), or long term, part time (e.g., 1–2 hours/session, one session/week, for 6 months to a year).

The provider guides the client in understanding what type of time frame is needed to achieve the program's goals and in recognizing the kind of schedule that is most appropriate for the participants.

Location is determined by the goals of the program and the needs of client and participants. If intense, fairly rapid training is needed, a full-time intensive *away* program, either in-country or in another country, may be the best choice. For part-time programs, on-site training is usually more convenient for participants and more cost effective for the client. On-site training works well when appropriate training space and equipment are available.

Off-site training, whether at the provider's facility or at another location, has the advantage of allowing participants to focus fully because they cannot be called away from training for work-related reasons. The time and inconvenience involved in traveling to an off-site training location may be disincentives to participation, however. Provider and client work together, with input from participants when necessary, to determine which location will best serve the needs of the training program.

The provider outlines the instructional mode for the program, whether traditional standup instruction, one-on-one tutoring, distance learning, self-instruction, or some combination of these. The provider then describes the ways in which technology can support the learning process, based on information from the client regarding the availability of different types of equipment. Technology-delivered instruction may include the use of audiotapes, telephones, videotapes, video cameras, CD-ROMs, Internet, satellite connections, and other multimedia options.

In conjunction with the description of ways in which technology will contribute to the program, provider and client identify the types and degree of resource support that the client can and will provide. Resource support includes training room and equipment setup; access to photocopying machines and educational supplies; the use of storage space between instructional sessions; and considerations for instructors, such as parking and building entry permits. Outlining the respective responsibilities of provider and client in the planning stage lays the groundwork for effective interaction while the program is taking place.

Progress Assessment and Reporting

The provider outlines a system for maintaining communication with client representatives as training proceeds. Regular communication allows provider and client to address logistical and attendance issues promptly, minimizing their effects. It also gives the provider opportunities to furnish informal progress reports. As training proceeds, participants' needs may change; the focus may narrow or broaden, or previously unrecognized needs may appear. Regular communication with the client allows the provider to report such changes immediately and explain any resulting adjustments to the curriculum.

The provider also outlines its timetable and mechanism for assessing the progress that participants are making in their development of work-related language skills. The timetable and mechanism may reflect legal considerations, such as labor laws and employee collective bargaining agreements that govern how and how often employee assessment may occur. Taking into account the client's wishes with regard to the use of standardized tests or the development of customized assessments, the provider notes how and how often some sort of formal assessment will take place and how the confidentiality of the results will be maintained.

Assessment of improvement often includes direct and indirect measures. Direct measures include greater breadth and depth of knowledge of work-related vocabulary, grammar, and language structure; higher efficiency in producing written material; and increased ability to understand and follow oral instructions. Direct assessment may be conducted by instructors who observe improvement in the classroom and by supervisors who observe specific language use in the workplace. Indirect measures include supervisor observations of overall improvement, positive customer feedback, and increased participant self-esteem. The focus of direct and indirect assessment is on the ways in which the skills that participants have learned have improved their on-the-job performance and contributed to the overall success of the company.

Program Evaluation

The workplace language training provider outlines the procedures that will be used to evaluate the program overall, taking into account any procedures that the client may use on a regular basis for evaluating training programs. Program evaluation involves a review of the original program goals and assessment of progress toward goal achievement; identification of other ways in which participants' improved language ability has had a positive impact; and ways in which logistical factors such as schedule, location, and use of technology supported or hindered the achievement of program goals.

Effective workplace language training providers seek to involve all stakeholders in the evaluation process, as they did in the program planning process, recognizing that participants, supervisors, and others who regularly interact with participants all have valuable insights to contribute. In addition, a provider may suggest the formation of an advisory committee to monitor progress and participate in final program evaluation.

An advisory or steering committee can provide oversight to ensure that a training program is maximally effective for the client, the participants, and the provider. Such a committee is most relevant in the case of a large program, a long-term program, or a program that will be replicated over a number of cycles. The committee's membership, responsibilities, and authority are spelled out jointly by the provider and the client in the planning stage. Typically, an advisory committee includes one member from each stakeholder group, and the committee's responsibilities include monitoring the satisfaction of all involved as the program progresses, reviewing evaluation forms, and collecting input on results when the program is finished.

Case Study 3.3: Provider Designs Workplace Literacy/ESOL Program Around Shift Schedule

A multinational corporation asked a workplace language training provider to design a combined workplace literacy/ESOL program for custodial staff at its corporate headquarters. The primary focus of the program was to be on reading skills; company management was motivated by the desire to provide literacy training as a benefit for these employees and to ensure that these workers could read labels, instructions, and safety warnings and complete brief work reports.

As the provider talked with the corporation's training manager and supervisors of potential program participants, several concerns surfaced. Because training would take place during participants' work hours, the schedule would need to accommodate their shift schedule: 7 am–3 pm, 3–11 pm, and 11 pm–7 am. The training schedule would also need to allow for a 2-week break at the end of December and a 4-week break in August, when most employees took their summer vacations.

When the provider raised the subject of size and makeup of the classes, the training manager expressed her understanding of the value of smaller classes, but was firm that she could not justify a class size of fewer than six participants, even if this meant mixing native and nonnative speakers, and possibly ability levels, in the same class. The manager also requested that the program be able to incorporate new participants on an ongoing basis.

Some supervisors noted that a similar training program had been tried several years earlier, with some problems. Workers who were not involved in the training had resented the fact that participants got time off to attend class, leaving their coworkers with more to do. In addition, a few employees had signed up for the program, then used the class time to take extended breaks from their job duties instead.

In designing a program for this client, the provider recognized that, from a logistical perspective, the shift schedule would have to form the foundation for its plan. From an instructional perspective, shorter class sessions would be more appropriate for these low-level learners and would also minimize their time away from the workplace.

The provider laid out a schedule in which participants would meet in two 90-minute class sessions per week. Training would run for 12 weeks (36 hours) in the fall and 12 weeks in the spring, with a break between for the December holiday. Training would run for 8 weeks (24 hours) in the summer, breaking for the August vacation period. Class sessions would take place at the beginning of each shift (7–8:30 am, 3–4:30 pm, and 11 pm–12:30 am) to catch participants when they were fresh. Class size would be kept to the minimum (six people) to allow instructors the flexibility to work with the differing skill levels and language backgrounds of participants.

continued on page 35

continued from page 34

The provider also specified that, after the assessment and placement of the initial group of participants, it would provide an assessment instrument that could be administered on an ad hoc basis by the training manager to employees who wished to enroll in the program later. The provider specified that new participants would be able to join the program only at the beginning and midpoint of each 12-week module and at the beginning of the 8-week module to minimize disruptions to continuing participants.

Finally, the provider outlined a plan for regular communication with the training manager and with supervisors for mutual feedback on participant progress and program operations. This regular contact would enable supervisors to be aware of and respond promptly to work conflicts, attendance problems, and any other matters that might arise.

Practice 3.4: Prepare and Submit a Proposal

The provider writes up the program design in the form of a proposal for the client. When writing a proposal for a private client organization, the provider adopts the proposal format that is appropriate for the client's country or culture, taking into account any legal requirements that may apply. In the case of a proposal written in response to a government or funding agency request for proposals (RFP), the provider follows the format mandated by the RFP instructions.

Effective workplace language training providers know and use the vocabulary of the business training world, that is, the vocabulary that corporate personnel managers and training directors expect to see. For example, providers speak of

- *instructors* or *training specialists,* not teachers

- *participants* or *trainees,* not students

- *training groups*, not classes or class groups

- *training sessions,* not classes

- *training rooms,* not classrooms

- *results* or *progress,* not grades or marks

Providers use company-specific language where possible and appropriate to refer to program participants, needs, and goals. They avoid the use of academic or research terms that may confuse or mystify client representatives.

Business Proposal

The provider may open the proposal with a statement of its capability and its philosophy of language training. This brief statement serves to set the context for the proposal itself. It allows the provider to make clear that its training programs aim to increase participants' ability to use language to improve job performance and that they are evaluated on the basis of the positive impact they have on job performance and corporate success.

The provider then states what it will do for the client. It outlines the program's goals and describes its plan of operation: how it will conduct instructional needs assessment and group participants; what instructional mode and technical resources it will use; where, when, and how often instruction will take place and how long the overall program will be; what the qualifications of the staff will be; how participant progress will be assessed; and how program evaluation will take place. The provider also outlines other aspects that it may have addressed with the client, such as frequency of client-provider meetings and constitution of an advisory committee.

The provider develops a budget that outlines costs for the training program, responding to the client's indications of the degree and type of cost breakdown it needs to see. The client may request a project price broken out into the individual components of instructional needs assessment, curriculum development, instruction, meetings, training materials, and indirect costs (overhead); or it may request an hourly rate with time projections. The provider accommodates the client's request to the extent possible within its own fiscal operating system.

Finally, the provider attaches references or letters of support to the proposal. When possible, the language training provider prepares an oral presentation to follow up on the written proposal and answer any questions that arise.

Response to RFPs

When responding to an agency's RFP, a provider does not usually have an opportunity to conduct an organizational needs assessment or interact at length with the potential client before submitting its proposal. The provider relies on the description of need that the agency provides in the RFP, augmenting that with any information that may be forthcoming at a vendor information session, if one is offered. In addition, the provider may approach the contact person designated in the RFP for answers to format or content questions.

Effective workplace language training providers follow a three-part procedure when submitting a bid in response to an RFP.

1. Follow the instructions for content, style, and format of the narrative, the budget, and other parts of the proposal.

2. Use the rating system specified in the RFP to determine the relative importance of different parts of the proposal and adjust level of effort accordingly.

3. Seek clarification from the contact person when uncertainty arises with regard to submission guidelines and other matters so that the finished proposal addresses as closely as possible the needs, objectives, and priorities of the soliciting agency.

Case Study 3.4: Provider Responds to Request for Proposals and Wins Government Contract

A U.S. government agency issued an RFP for an ESL oral communication skills program for government employees. The issuing agency was the training center for a federal department, and, as such, drew participants for its training programs from all divisions of the department. Rather than maintain a staff of trainers, the training center contracted with external providers for the development and provision of training programs. The agency itself furnished classroom space and equipment.

A workplace language training provider decided to bid for the contract. The provider noted that the RFP specified an initial placement process that would result in division of potential participants into class groups by proficiency level. Although the provider would have preferred to divide groups according to job task, the provider agreed to the RFP constraints and outlined the assessment process it would use for placement and the instructional curricula for the class groups that would result.

At the information session offered by the agency, the provider learned that the agency's issuance of the RFP was the result of multiple requests from internal sources, including upper level managers who wanted the training for their staff members and lower level managers and administrative assistants who wanted the training for themselves. No explicit information about the potential participants' cultural or linguistic backgrounds was forthcoming.

On the basis of this information, the provider outlined a proposed program that included initial assessment and instruction for three participant groups. For the assessment, the provider planned to audiotape individual oral interviews of 10 minutes' duration. The interviewer would ask open-ended questions that encouraged the potential participant to talk about work tasks and work-related language use. In this way, the assessment interviews would double as a partial instructional needs assessment.

The provider then outlined instructional curricula for participant groups at three levels. Guessing that secretarial staff and lower level managers would place into each group, and drawing on its experience with similar program participants, the provider created a sequence of topic areas for each curriculum that began with core business communication needs and a fairly structured set of activities and moved to topics suggested by participants and a more flexible structure as the program progressed. This sequence allowed time for participants' needs to surface and for the provider to develop learning activities to address them.

The provider won the contract, and the success of its programs led to extension of the contract for a second year.

Practice 3.5: Negotiate the Contract

Once the client has reviewed and accepted the proposal, contract negotiation takes place. Negotiation may involve modification of the proposal to meet needs that have become evident since the original client-provider meetings took place or to clarify or modify specific aspects of the provider's operating plan. Negotiation may also involve discussion of costs and ways of containing them.

Effective workplace language training providers maintain a flexible and responsive approach throughout the negotiation process and seek to accommodate client needs. They have also identified the essential requirements of a quality workplace language training program and can articulate those for clients to indicate the point beyond which compromise is unacceptable.

In working with a client to move from proposal to contract, a provider may employ one or more strategies for accommodating client needs.

- The provider may propose a two-step process, with one contract to cover conducting the instructional needs assessment and developing the program's instructional design, and a second to cover the actual delivery of the program. The second contract would not be drawn up until the activities covered by the first had been completed. The results of the detailed instructional needs assessment might show some ways in which the instructional program could be adjusted to reduce costs.

- The provider may present a proposal with alternatives, such as shorter and longer training programs with corresponding differences in expected outcomes.

- The provider may suggest a series of small contracts for clients with complex procedural requirements for contracts over a certain amount. Dividing the larger program so that there are separate contracts for needs assessment, materials design, the first month of instruction, the second month of instruction, and so on can facilitate the contracting process for client and provider.

When provider and client come to agreement on terms, the contract is drawn up, with payment terms and a provision for revision if new information surfaces or contingencies that require rescheduling arise after the contract is signed.

There is no such thing as a standard contract that applies across the wide range of program types and settings worldwide. Contracts range in size from a one-page memorandum to a 100-page document negotiated by two teams of lawyers, one representing the provider, the other representing the client. In some cultures, formal contracts are not considered binding, and negotiations may continue throughout the life of the project. In other cultures, agreements are made orally. In such cases, following up with a letter of intent, confirming the details of the oral communication, would be considered a minimally acceptable practice.

Case Study 3.5: Provider Accommodates Agency Writing Program's Budget Constraints During Contract Negotiation

A workplace language training provider had worked for several weeks with the head of a department within a U.S. federal agency to develop a writing program for department employees. Following the organizational needs assessment, the provider and the client had agreed that the provider would begin by administering a written placement test. The results of the test would serve as data for the instructional needs assessment and also enable the provider to group employees by job and proficiency level. The provider anticipated that the placement process would result in four groups: a higher and a lower level for administrative assistants and a higher and a lower level for entry-level managerial staff.

When the provider and the client began to negotiate the contract, however, the department head presented a new problem. She had called the provider because the head of the agency had issued an order requiring all departments to demonstrate improvement in employee writing skills within 12 months. However, she only had discretionary authority to issue contracts for $5,000 or less; contracts over that amount were subject to a lengthy approval process. The only way for the department head to meet the agency head's 12-month deadline was to circumvent the approval process for large contracts and get started with training right away. In fact, although the new fiscal year was about to begin, the department head had a small amount of money remaining in the current year's training budget, and she hoped to use that for the initial phase of the training.

The provider responded by offering to create one contract just for the design and administration of the instructional needs assessment. This contract could be drawn up immediately and the work completed fairly quickly, enabling the client to use the funds remaining in the current year's budget.

The provider also offered to wait to draw up contracts for the actual training until the needs assessment had been reviewed and the potential participants divided into groups. Then, an individual contract could be drawn up for each class group. In this way, the entire training program could be provided without any one contract exceeding the $5,000 discretionary limit.

In the short run, this solution addressed the client's needs and made it possible for the program to get underway immediately. In the long run, it set up a structure that opened the door to further training. Having individual contracts for each class group helped the client to think about the needs of each group independently of the others and to agree to sponsor a continuation of training for two of the groups when the original program ended.

▓ Conclusion

From contact to contract, the building process that results in a successful client relationship can be lengthy, and the time dedicated to it is not directly compensated. Effective workplace language training providers are willing to invest this time, recognizing the return that will come later in the form of successful programs, repeat business, and recommendations to other potential clients.

Effective Practice 4

The Workplace Language Training Provider Provides Quality Program Staff and Appropriate Staff Support

Overview

An effective workplace language training provider is able to provide quality staffing for its programs. During the organizational needs assessment and program development process, provider and client have determined the levels of instructional staffing, management staffing, and administrative support that will be appropriate for a given program. Depending on the size and goals of the training program, staffing may include a program manager, a curriculum specialist, an assessment specialist, and instructors.

To staff the program, the provider then selects individuals whose experience and qualifications will make them a good match for the client and the training participants. Effective workplace language training providers have set minimum qualifications for instructors, which usually include a combination of academic work and relevant experience. Qualifications for program managers typically include experience and training in program supervision.

To attract and retain a strong staff, the workplace language training provider provides appropriate compensation and effective support, including administrative support and in-service training opportunities. Such support ensures that the provider's staff have current knowledge of training theory and praxis and the ability to function efficiently while providing workplace language training. Providing such support entails three practices.

Practice 4.1: determine necessary staffing level and administrative structure of the program

Practice 4.2: recruit and select qualified staff

Practice 4.3: provide appropriate and effective staff support and development

Practice 4.1: Determine Necessary Staffing Level and Administrative Structure of the Program

The level of staffing for a program depends on factors determined during the organizational needs assessment and contract negotiation process, including program size and complexity, program location (on or off site), and type and availability of funding. In some cases, only one language trainer is needed, whereas in others, grant requirements or corporate commitments call for a more complex structure that may include a program director, a curriculum coordinator, several instructors, an assessment specialist, and support staff.

Where a client envisions the establishment of a long-term or ongoing training program, or where training is to involve the communication of specialized work-related knowledge in addition to language instruction, client employees may become part of the staff team. Employees whose role is to impart technical knowledge can be scheduled into the curriculum as guest speakers, with provider staff creating class activities to support their presentations. Employees who are to become part of an ongoing training system can serve in a tutorial capacity, first receiving orientation and training and then working independently with individual learners in or out of the classroom.

In every case, the goal of the language training provider is to furnish the level and kind of staffing and support that will ensure a quality program that meets or exceeds client objectives and expectations. The provider and the client work together to identify a staffing level that will provide a quality program within the financial parameters defined by the client.

Staffing is described here in terms of staff functions. Whether multiple functions require multiple staff or can be assigned to one or two individuals depends on the size and complexity of a particular workplace language training program, its location (on or off site), and the administrative structure of the workplace language training provider.

Program Management

Program management includes critical oversight and coordination functions. The program management role may involve coordinating functions at a single site or overseeing site coordinators who carry out managerial functions at several sites. The program manager acts as the provider's chief liaison with the client organization, coordinates the program schedule, supervises program staff, develops reports, manages the budget, and oversees program evaluation.

When a program involves multiple class groups or levels of instruction conducted by several instructors, the program management function may be carried out by a manager who is hired specifically for the program and whose salary is part of the program's direct costs. This is often the case with programs that are conducted on site. With smaller on-site programs, one of the instructors may be designated as the program manager. Alternatively, whether a program is conducted on site or at the training provider's site, program management may be handled by a member of the provider's administrative staff.

Curriculum Development and Coordination

Curriculum coordination ensures that individual class curricula are consonant with one another and that transitions between modules are smooth. The curriculum coordinator evaluates the results of the organizational and instructional needs assessments and uses that information to develop program content and training materials that will address the client's objectives for the training. The curriculum coordinator also monitors the curriculum regularly and modifies it as needed.

In small programs, the instructor or instructors generally assume the role of curriculum coordinator. When a program involves multiple class groups or levels of instruction conducted by several instructors, curriculum coordination becomes a large enough task to require the assignment of a staff person specifically for this function. With language training programs that involve relatively few class groups or levels, the curriculum coordination function may be assigned to the program manager. Alternatively, program instructors may take on this function as a team.

Language Training

The language training function is to plan and teach classes and keep records of attendance and progress. Instructors work with one another and with the curriculum coordinator to adjust the curriculum in response to the needs that become evident as instruction progresses. Instructors report general issues and individual participant problems to the program manager and work with the program manager and client representatives to resolve them. Finally, instructors develop and administer authentic assessments of participant progress, or work with the assessment specialist to do so.

Recruitment and qualifications of instructors are discussed under Practice 4.2 below.

Assessment

Assessment includes development, administration, and scoring of tests and reporting of test results at three stages: the initial instructional needs assessment and participant placement testing; assessments of participant progress at designated points during the course of instruction (formative evaluation); and the assessment of overall participant progress as of the program's end (summative evaluation).

When the use of standardized tests is mandated by government funding agencies or client objectives, testing procedures may require that a trained assessment specialist be retained to supervise administration and scoring. In cases where provider and client have agreed on the use of customized workplace-related placement, proficiency and achievement tests instead of or in addition to standardized assessments, the development, administration, scoring, and reporting roles will be assigned to provider staff. The development role, which involves customizing assessment instruments so that they correspond with the language functions of a specific workplace, should be assigned to a staff person who has a background in test development and scoring and can therefore ensure that the customized assessments will provide valid, reliable results.

Program Evaluation

Program evaluation is a critical and ongoing component of any workplace language training program. Program evaluation usually involves the collaborative efforts of program managers and staff and an external program evaluator. See Effective Practice 9 for a more complete discussion of this core component.

> ### Case Study 4.1: Provider Builds Appropriate Staffing and Administration Into Workplace Literacy/ESOL Program
>
> The workplace literacy/ESOL program for custodial employees described in the previous chapter (Case Study 3.3) presented several staffing challenges for the workplace language training provider. Although the client had conducted an informal survey of employees to assess interest levels, until workers actually made a commitment and took the initial assessment, the provider did not know how many participants or class groups there would be in each work shift. In addition, the provider had to find instructors who were willing to teach early in the morning, in the middle of the afternoon, and late at night. In order to maintain communication with the training manager, who worked a regular 9–5 day, the provider had to have a mechanism for collecting information from the instructors and conveying it during normal business hours.
>
> The provider began by designating an experienced member of its regular administrative staff to serve as the program manager. This manager would conduct the initial assessment, administering the test, scoring it, and determining class groupings. The manager would also coordinate the development of the curriculum and instructional materials for the program and work with instructors to ensure that the materials were meeting participants' needs. During the instructional program, the manager would be the main point of contact for the instructors and the client. Instructors would report successes, problems, and attendance on a weekly basis, and the manager would collect all the information and pass it on to the client's training manager.
>
> The provider then began recruiting instructors to teach in the program. A local retired schoolteachers' group proved a good source of instructors for the early morning and mid-afternoon slots; the provider was able to find three teachers with ESL credentials. A former teacher, currently working for a research organization, also indicated interest in teaching an early morning class before her regular workday. Finding instructors for the night slot proved more challenging, but the provider turned to the local university and found that several graduate students in a MATESOL program were interested.
>
> For the first 12-week module, the provider ended up hiring six instructors for seven class groups: three at 7 am, two at 3 pm, and two at 11 pm. One of the retired teachers, who lived near the client's corporate headquarters, took a 7 am and a 3 pm class. The other former teachers each took one 7 am or 3 pm class, and two graduate students took the two 11 pm classes.

▤ Practice 4.2: Recruit and Select Qualified Staff

Qualifications

Effective workplace language training requires staff who are cognizant of the culture of the workplace and knowledgeable about language teaching methodology for adult ESL/EFL learners. Qualifications for instructors therefore include a combination of an academic degree in English language teaching and experience in the world of work, either as an instructor or in another role.

There is no worldwide agreement on the ideal minimum educational preparation for persons serving as instructors, program managers, and curriculum coordinators. In some countries, a master's or equivalent degree in TESOL or applied linguistics is the suggested level and kind of preparation. In other areas of the world, a University of Cambridge Examinations Syndicate

Diploma in English Language Teaching to Adults (UCLES DELTA, formerly the Royal Society of Arts diploma) is acceptable and even preferable to a master's degree because it includes practical preparation in lesson planning, teaching techniques, and classroom management.

Although it has been customary to require near-native proficiency in English, adherence to this qualification is not always necessary. Instructors from linguistic and cultural backgrounds similar to those of program participants can provide valuable cross-cultural and contrastive insights, as well as bilingual explanations when necessary.

In addition to professional preparation, effective workplace language training providers usually require an appropriate level of experience, particularly for program managers and instructors who will train client employees as tutors. Most importantly, these providers recognize that, although formal training gives an ESL professional an important knowledge base for use in training situations, successful instructors are distinguished as much by personal qualities as by background. These qualities include

- a willingness to become familiar with the client organization's operations, products or services, and needs

- loyalty to the provider organization

- demonstrated care for and rapport with program participants

- the belief that participants are also clients

- the ability to act as an effective liaison between provider and client

- the ability to work independently without constant supervision

- the ability to be flexible when working in less-than-ideal conditions

- sensitivity to the concerns of adults who may be apprehensive about training

- an awareness of the standards of dress and behavior appropriate for the workplace context

In recruiting and hiring staff, effective workplace language training providers may accept (under certain circumstances) relevant experience or non-ESL-specific teaching qualifications in order to secure program staff who they believe will provide the best possible service to a client. These providers recognize that, with appropriate guidance, a teaching professional with a different academic background or type of experience can become a highly skilled workplace language trainer.

Recruitment

Although staff are often recruited informally (i.e., by word of mouth), an effective recruiting plan also includes advertising in local newspapers, education- and business-related publications, radio and television, and online venues. Advertisements can also be placed at universities, adult education centers, schools, social service agencies, labor organizations, businesses, and professional conferences. Providers may also advertise through state, provincial, and regional public agencies. The advertisement should contain the position title and duties, required minimum qualifications, start date, salary or salary range, and application instructions (e.g., cover letter, résumé, and references).

In programs funded by government or other public sector grants, or even housed in public sector institutions, specific guidelines, such as affirmative action and equal opportunity in the United States, must sometimes be followed when recruiting staff. Such programs require evidence that positions have been advertised widely and that all qualified applicants have been given fair consideration. In addition, some cultures may dictate qualifications based on age, gender, sexual orientation, religion, and nationality. In such situations, providers have the responsibility to consider whether such criteria violate ethical principles and balance that consideration with the potential benefits of pursuing the contract. Workplace language training providers must also be aware of any governmental regulations related to the hiring of staff from outside the country.

When interviewing potential employees, a workplace language training provider may request that the potential employee conduct a short demonstration lesson or answer work-related hypothetical questions. Demonstrations give providers an effective way to identify applicants with the skills and personal qualities that they are seeking, and asking applicants hypothetical situation questions can help to reveal their knowledge, competence, and resourcefulness for performing effectively in the workplace environment.

Compensation

The appropriate type and level of compensation for instructors, program managers, and other staff varies from country to country as well as within countries. Compensation levels also often vary among providers in the same location. Effective workplace language training providers are aware of the pay scales that are typical for salaried and contract employees in the areas in which they do business and seek to position themselves at the higher end of the scale in order to attract and retain quality staff members.

Effective workplace language training providers also recognize that compensation is not only about money; it also includes the intangible factors that contribute to employee satisfaction. These providers create environments in which instructors and other staff can take on challenging and interesting assignments, obtain the administrative and professional development support they need, and experience success in meeting the goals of the programs in which they are involved. Such an environment is one that attracts quality instructors and encourages them to stay with the organization.

▓ Practice 4.3: Provide Appropriate and Effective Staff Support and Development

The success of workplace language training depends on the ability of program staff to provide instruction that leads to the achievement of client objectives. This means that, in addition to hiring qualified staff, the language training provider must furnish appropriate and effective staff support. Such support includes administrative support and professional development opportunities. An effective support system has the additional advantage of enabling a provider to retain highly qualified staff members.

Staff Support

Counseling and Referral Services
There is not complete agreement about the necessity for counseling in workplace language training, but a counselor who is trained in cross-cultural communication and cognizant of the special needs of program participants can be a valuable asset. This is especially true in ESL situations where immigrant workers are dealing with an unfamiliar culture and legal system as well as a new language.

For workers from some cultural backgrounds, the title *counselor* may carry a stigma, so an alternate title, such as *career advisor*, may be preferable. A counselor or career advisor can address workers' total development and well-being by

- assisting with securing any child-care and transportation support services offered by the institution or program

- making referrals to social service, immigration, medical, and education or training organizations

- providing career assessment and development

- providing advice about culturally appropriate workplace behavior

In on-site training programs, the role of counselor is generally filled by staff in the human resources or personnel department. However, whether a program takes place on or off site, an effective workplace language training provider seeks to ensure that counseling is available, either from a designated person or through a referral system, to program participants who need it.

Because the possible functions of a counselor in workplace language training can vary widely, it is difficult to pinpoint specific qualifications for this role. A higher education degree in counseling, social work, industrial relations or human resources; workplace experience in cross-cultural communication; and familiarity with local service providers are recommended. Where most or all program participants come from the same language background, the ability to communicate with them in their first language can be an asset.

Technical Assistance

Occasionally, an external consultant may be used to assist program instructors with complex instructional technology, such as programming computer-assisted language lessons or making video- or audiotapes of workplace English lessons for broadcast or home use.

Office Assistance

The office assistance function includes assisting with program logistics, class scheduling, and record keeping; purchasing supplies; scheduling training, staff, and other meetings and appointments; and making copies of class materials. In on-site programs, this type of support is provided by a designated employee of the client, often a staff person in the human resources or personnel department. With programs conducted at the provider's site, the office assistance function is handled by a member of the provider's staff, often an administrative assistant who also responds to inquiries about the provider's program(s), does financial record keeping, and maintains personnel and other records.

Intake/Admissions

Workplace language training providers who conduct large programs at their own sites often have one or more admissions clerks. These staff members make sure that participants have the required documentation and basic qualifications to be admitted to the program and help them complete admissions information forms. The admissions clerk may also administer written placement tests that do not require administration by a specialist. A bilingual person is suggested for this function if most participants come from the same language background.

Intake/admission may also take place directly at the workplace (i.e., on site).

Professional Development Opportunities

Professional development for program staff is also a critical component and may be provided informally or formally, with existing program staff or by engaging external consultants, or through a combination of these.

Internal Professional Development Options

Internal professional development options give staff the opportunity to get to know one another, build on one another's skills and strengths, and develop an identity as a team. These options include orientations, staff meetings and joint planning time, in-service training, and resource centers.

Orientations help staff become acquainted and establish program coordination and communication procedures. They also give new staff perspective on the provider organization's standards and expectations for its employees.

Regularly scheduled staff meetings promote effective communication and coordination, which is probably the single most critical form of staff support. Staff meetings should take place every 1–2 weeks. This schedule will allow instructors to work with the program manager, curriculum coordinator, and counselor or career advisor on resolution of problematic areas before these get out of hand. Regularly scheduled joint planning time allows instructors to ensure that the curriculum develops cohesively across different class groups and skill levels and that ongoing formative evaluation takes place in a consistent way. By working together, staff draw on one another's knowledge and experience and all become more effective providers of the services that clients seek.

In-service training, whether provided by a staff member or an external consultant, can be an effective way to develop or improve specific skills. In-service training often ranges from 3–6 hours per day and can be delivered in an intensive 1–5-day format or in weekly or monthly intervals.

In-service training topics may include further development of multilevel teaching techniques, adapting workplace materials for language training, authentic assessment of learner skills and progress, integrating technology into workplace language training, adapting existing materials to the requirements of workplace language training, and understanding the culture of the workplace. This type of training can help instructors broaden and deepen their understanding of the training needs associated with specific types of businesses and industries and also enhance their ability to accomplish workplace language training program goals.

In-service training can also include in-class observation, in which a colleague or the program manager observes the instructor in action and makes notes for later review and discussion. In some countries, individuals who participate in in-service training may receive university credit through a continuing education program at a local university. Research suggests that in-service training is especially effective if the trainer can return to monitor how effectively the newly learned skills have been implemented.

A workplace language training provider may also establish a resource center where instructors, curriculum coordinators, and program managers can plan lessons and prepare materials. Such resource centers usually include a library of reference books and off-the-shelf texts, instructional materials and classroom activities developed for previous workplace language training programs, and resources for professional development.

External Professional Development Options
These include membership in professional organizations such as Teachers of English to Speakers of Other Languages (TESOL) and International Association of Teachers of English as a Foreign Language (IATEFL) and attendance at professional conferences. Institutional memberships in these associations allow language training providers to extend staff support opportunities through professional publications and online discussion forums and bulletin boards. When funding is not available to support staff attendance at professional organizations' annual meetings, participation in affiliate regional, state, or local conferences can be more accessible.

Case Study 4.3: Language School in Ecuador Creates Workplace English Department

A language school in Ecuador experienced a dramatic increase in the number of contracts to teach English in companies and government organizations. The school, however, had trouble fitting this workplace component into its existing schedule. For the majority of the workplace contracts, the trainer taught in the workplace for only part of the day, which meant that the trainer then taught general English classes back at the school for the remainder of the day. Coordinating the on-site and in-school parts of these teachers' schedules proved problematic because many clients requested that workplace language training take place in the late afternoon, when most classes at the language school took place.

In addition to the scheduling issues, the school experienced a number of logistical problems. Instructors did not always have the materials or equipment they needed, and there was no established way for them to report either to the school or to the clients while training programs were in progress. Communication among instructors, school, and clients was often haphazard, which meant that problems that could have been resolved quickly were instead allowed to continue.

To address this situation, the language school created a workplace English department with its own staff of instructors, some part time and some full time, who could meet the demands of workplace scheduling without reference to the in-school schedule. The school hired a department director to be responsible for overall program coordination and communication with clients. In addition, to the great relief of the instructors, the school hired two program assistants for the department, one to purchase and deliver equipment and materials to the work site and solve minor on-site problems, and the other to take care of inquiries, handle routine office tasks, and reproduce materials. The office assistants were also expected to organize needs assessment and placement testing, keep relevant participant records, and see that the appropriate records and reports were sent to the client.

This structural change improved the situation for everyone. The director of the school no longer had to juggle competing schedules when making teacher assignments. Instructors could still take advantage of the resources available to them at the school, but could focus on instructional strategies appropriate to the workplace setting. Most important of all, clients saw a marked improvement in the provider's responsiveness to their needs.

▦ Conclusion

In the matter of staffing for its programs, an effective workplace language training provider recognizes that a strong relationship with its client and a strong relationship with its staff go hand in hand. The provider seeks to identify the instructors and other staff who are best equipped to meet the client's needs, goals, and expectations. At the same time, the provider creates an environment for the staff that promotes their ability to succeed. Creation of such an environment enables the provider to set high expectations for its staff and know that those expectations will be met.

Effective Practice 5

The Workplace Language Training Provider Conducts a Comprehensive Research-Based Instructional Needs Assessment

Overview

The most effective workplace language training programs are based on a thorough assessment of the needs of program participants. The purpose of the assessment is to determine how communicative competence (see Introduction) in the workplace is defined and what participants' levels of competence are. That is, assessment discovers the difference between what participants are currently able to do with language (*Present Situation Analysis*, or PSA) and what they need to be able to do (*Target Situation Analysis*, or TSA). With this information, the workplace language training provider is able to develop a task-based instructional curriculum with materials and activities that promote development of the language skills participants need to perform effectively on the job.

The first part of the needs assessment involves making observations in order to identify and analyze effective task-related language use in the workplace. Information is also collected from participants' supervisors, managers, and colleagues through interviews or questionnaires. The workplace language training provider combines the data gathered in these observations with the information provided by client representatives during the organizational needs assessment to create a full, client-specific picture of the objectives for the instructional program.

The second part of the needs assessment involves administering a written language skill assessment or individual oral interviews, as appropriate, to determine participants' current levels of proficiency. These assessments are workplace and task specific; they are based on the information gathered in the first part of the needs assessment, and they are designed to enable the provider to gauge the difference between the target proficiency (TSA) and participants' current proficiency (PSA). The assessments also give the provider an opportunity to solicit input from participants themselves regarding the needs they perceive for their own language skill development.

Client representatives may resist the idea of committing time and money to an instructional needs assessment, believing that an experienced provider should be able to gather sufficient information from the organizational needs assessment and a standardized proficiency test. Effective workplace language training providers are able to demonstrate to their clients the direct connections between thorough information gathering of the type described here and targeted instruction that ensures that participants will gain the skills they need to perform tasks effectively in the workplace. Implementation of an instructional needs assessment involves five practices.

Practice 5.1: define the rationale and framework for the assessment

Practice 5.2: involve all stakeholders in the assessment process

Practice 5.3: collect and analyze data on language use in the workplace

Practice 5.4: collect data on the oral and written language proficiency of (potential) participants

Practice 5.5: report the results of the instructional needs assessment to the client

Practice 5.1: Define the Rationale and Framework for the Assessment

During the organizational needs assessment and discussion of the proposal, the client and the provider have articulated the goals for the training program: what program participants should know and be able to do with language when training concludes. These goals dictate the rationale and framework for the instructional needs assessment.

The framework states what the provider will do and to whom. The rationale explains why. For example, if the goal of the program is to enable systems analysts to write clear, concise reports, the provider will examine acceptable reports and gather input from analysts and their superiors to determine what makes an acceptable report (TSA). The provider will also assess potential participants' current writing ability to determine the extent of the gap between participants' current skill levels (PSA) and the skill levels required for producing acceptable reports. The provider will also discuss other types of writing assignments that systems analysts currently have or might have when their language skills improve in order to develop an instructional program that fully addresses participant and client needs.

The framework for the first part of the assessment depends on how much information was gathered during the organizational needs assessment phase. Building on the information gained in the earlier stage, the workplace language training provider identifies areas in which it needs further input and the types of individuals (e.g., supervisors, managers, coworkers) who can provide that input. The framework for this part of the assessment is also guided by practical consideration of the most efficient way(s) to gather needed information. For some clients, written questionnaires are preferable, whereas for others, brief oral interviews work best. In some situations, on-the-job observations may be appropriate.

The framework for the second part of the assessment depends on the skills to be assessed. Reading and writing skills assessments can be administered to participants as a group; oral skills assessments require one-on-one interviews. Even when a program is to focus exclusively on reading and writing, however, a careful assessment includes individual interviews in which potential participants can talk about their own perceptions of their needs and abilities.

Whatever the goals of the program, the needs assessment process is shaped by three fundamental questions:

1. What functions and tasks does the employee need to do?

2. What language competencies are required to do those functions and tasks well? (TSA)

3. How does the employee currently do those functions and tasks? (PSA)

This pragmatic, tool-based view of English is a fundamental characteristic of effective workplace language training providers (see the discussion of task-based instruction in the Introduction). It distinguishes them from academic English instructors, who think of language as an art form and see mastery of English as an end in itself.

Case Study 5.1: Provider Aligns Writing Task With Assessment Rationale and Framework

For the department of a U.S. federal agency described in Case Study 3.6, where employees needed to improve their writing skills, the workplace language training provider needed to conduct an instructional needs assessment of the written language needs and abilities of administrative assistants and entry-level managers. The framework for assessment of potential participants' PSA was fairly straightforward: The provider used a customized written test on which potential participants completed tasks that mimicked those they carried out in the workplace and then wrote about their own perceptions of their language training needs. The provider also asked potential participants' supervisors to complete brief written questionnaires on which they described the training needs that they perceived and reported any feedback on potential participants' writing skills that they had received from outside sources.

The rationale for this framework was that participants and their immediate supervisors were best equipped to describe the types of writing that were done on the job and the training needs that related to them. Comments and feedback from people outside the department were available only in anecdotal form and so had to be collected from the supervisors.

The framework for the TSA was slightly more complex. The original motivation for the training program had been a directive from the head of the agency stating that all employees should be able to write in "plain English" by the end of the coming fiscal year. In addition to collecting samples of writing that illustrated the target skill level, therefore, the workplace language training provider had to discover what the agency head meant by "plain English" and make that definition a part of the training target. This involved interviews with higher level agency personnel outside the department that had originally requested the training and subsequent integration of the information gained into the TSA.

Practice 5.2: Involve all Stakeholders in the Assessment Process

Input from all stakeholders is essential to the creation of a full, accurate picture of language use in the workplace. The workplace language training provider begins with the information gained during the organizational needs assessment, identifies stakeholders who have not yet provided input, and develops appropriate methods for obtaining their contributions.

Depending on the organizational structure and the business focus of the client, the list of stakeholders may include the human resources director, the training manager, department heads and supervisors, senior management, customers, participants' coworkers, and the potential participants themselves. The point is not for colleagues, supervisors, and others to report on specific individuals. Rather, the provider asks these stakeholders to describe, on the basis of their experience, the ways in which language is used in the workplace and the ways in which communication could improve. What English language skills does an individual need to possess in order to perform effectively in this specific workplace? What have been the observable effects of language limitations?

Involving potential participants' superiors, whether supervisors or upper management, in the needs assessment is beneficial for two reasons. First, these people can provide important insights into the language skills participants need to master in order to perform their jobs effectively and the opportunities for growth and advancement that could be available to them as their English improves. Second, giving input helps supervisors and managers understand the program and become committed to its success and the success of those who participate in it.

The provider may be able to shadow and interview employees, including potential program participants and workers who are competent speakers of English. Observation and interviewing of potential participants gives the provider information about current English skills levels (PSA) and the impact of language limitations on workplace effectiveness. Observation and interviewing of coworkers who are competent speakers of English gives the provider information on the skills participants need to master (TSA).

Case Study 5.2: Providers in Somali Refugee Organization Widen Scope of Data Collection to Include all Stakeholders in Program

A private voluntary organization was asked to design a program for secretaries at the Somali Refugee Health Unit of the Somali Extraordinary Commission for Refugees in the early 1980s. During the organizational needs assessment, the client representative stated that the secretaries needed to use English to answer the phone, take messages, and write memos and letters. During the instructional needs assessment, interviews with potential participants confirmed that these were the tasks that they were expected to perform.

When the provider involved the doctors who headed the various departments, however, an expanded picture emerged. The doctors recognized the importance of the job tasks described, but stated that they also wanted the secretaries' English to improve so that the secretaries would be able to take minutes at department meetings. The minute-taking function had not been mentioned by either the client representative or the potential participants. Involving the department heads in the instructional needs assessment enabled the provider to identify not only the secretaries' current duties but also this other task that might be assigned to them as their English improved. As a result, the provider was able to develop an instructional program that addressed current and potential job duties and met the needs of all stakeholders.

▤ Practice 5.3: Collect and Analyze Data on Language Use in the Workplace

The workplace language training provider identifies the types of data to collect and selects collection strategies based on the framework and rationale for the instructional needs assessment. Strategies may include person-to-person or telephone interviews, questionnaires, observation on

Case Study 5.3: Provider Working With Hotel Employees Uses Data Analysis to Develop Successful Materials

A private ESL consultant was working with a hotel in a large U.S. city to develop a workplace English training program for hotel housekeepers. During the organizational needs assessment, hotel representatives had told the provider that one of the housekeepers' responsibilities was to communicate by telephone with various departments in the hotel. The housekeepers were expected to use the telephone to request pickup of room service trays, report broken fixtures, and follow up on other guest needs.

The housekeepers did not have the language skills they needed to make these telephone calls successfully. The hotel had developed video materials to train hotel employees to interact politely with others in person and on the telephone. The personnel manager had used the video with the housekeepers, but the housekeepers were still unable to make telephone requests for service. When they tried, confusion resulted, other employees' time was wasted, and guests complained about the hotel's failure to follow up on problems.

Viewing the video, the provider saw that it focused on polite openings and closings for telephone communication, an important feature of communication with guests. Observing the housekeepers on the job, the provider noted that employee-to-employee requests for service involved a different language task than employee-to-guest communication. In employee-to-employee communication tasks, efficiency was most important; polite language was irrelevant because all employees knew the importance of rapid response to call-in requests. In some cases, in fact, the polite language actually caused confusion on the part of the employees receiving the housekeepers' calls.

On the basis of this needs assessment, the provider developed a series of model conversations that participants practiced. He then had participants role play situations in which they had to choose appropriate language for communicating a request for service. The first breakthrough was made when the provider, conducting another observation, encouraged a housekeeper to phone in an actual request for assistance. She did so, and as she hung up the phone she burst into excited laughter over her success.

the job, collection of print materials used on the job, and collection of written materials that exemplify the writing skills that the client wants its employees to possess. The provider is careful to maintain confidentiality when disclosure of a source of information would compromise the project or someone's position.

To analyze the data it has collected, the workplace language training provider categorizes it according to genres, themes, functions, and tasks. Genres are forms of communication (written or spoken) that are recognized by an established group or community as having a specific purpose and distinguishing features. Themes are broad-brush labels for work-related communication activities, such as participating in meetings, writing technical reports, or communicating on an assembly line. Functions are the specific reasons for which language is used: to greet, to complain, to give instructions, to ask for clarification. A task, as noted in the Introduction, is an action that is accomplished through the use of language. A task is a function plus the conditions that surround it: who it is done with or to and whether it is spoken or written, planned or spontaneous, relatively brief or relatively lengthy, and other conditions.

Once the provider has identified the themes, tasks, and functions that are characteristic of language use in the client workplace, it can identify patterns that emerge and tasks or functions that occur across themes. For example, the function of asking for clarification can occur as part of the theme "participating in meetings" and the theme "handling customer complaints." Its recognition of emergent patterns, important themes, and recurring functions and tasks gives the workplace language training provider the foundation for identifying topics for instruction and setting them in priority order. This process is also referred to as a language audit.

▤ Practice 5.4: Collect Data on the Oral and Written Language Proficiency of Potential Participants

The workplace language training provider assesses oral and written English language skills, depending on the rationale and framework for the instructional needs assessment. Potential participants' listening and speaking skills are best assessed in individual interviews in which the workplace language training provider can use a combination of questions and exercises to discover needs for work on pronunciation and intonation as well as vocabulary, grammar, and ability to use context-specific language.

These individual interviews also provide excellent opportunities for eliciting potential program participants' own needs and goals for training. Sometimes participants find it difficult to be precise about their needs; in such cases, the interviewer can assist by asking about specific communication situations the employee encounters in the workplace and about things the employee has difficulty in understanding or handling.

Assessment of reading and writing skills is done with an assessment that reflects the types of reading and writing the employee does on the job. Employees may also submit samples of actual work-related writing tasks and written answers to questions about their own goals for language skill development.

When a written assessment instrument (test) is used, it may be an instrument designed by the workplace language training provider, a standardized instrument, or some combination of the two. Use of a standardized instrument is appropriate only when that instrument is designed for a specific work level or field or when it consists of communication tasks that are similar to those that take place in participants' workplace, and the range of proficiency levels is appropriate to the goals of the client and the current skills of the program participants. Effective workplace language training providers prefer to develop client-specific assessment instruments because these provide a more accurate picture of participants' actual PSA with respect to their jobs. They therefore are more useful to a provider who needs to identify the gaps between PSA and TSA in order to construct an effective instructional program. They also provide a relevant basis for evaluation of participant progress as instruction takes place.

▤ Practice 5.5: Report the Results of the Instructional Needs Assessment to the Client

It is relatively easy to provide an informal oral report to the client on the results of the needs assessment. Respect for the client organization can be shown by taking the time to put together a formal written report, however. Such a report can enable management to see the areas of need more precisely and relate them to specific communication skills, which it might not have been able to do earlier.

Case Study 5.4: Provider Collects Oral and Written Data on Nurses for Program in Persian Gulf Hospital

A new hospital was being built in one of the Persian Gulf states, and employees were being recruited from a variety of nationalities and language backgrounds. The official language of communication in the hospital among employees at all levels would be English. The hospital wanted to hire some experienced nurses whose English was not strong enough to assure that they would be able to communicate successfully in this environment, so a workplace language training firm was brought in to design a program for these nurses.

In the initial phase of the instructional needs assessment, the provider determined that the nurses needed to be able to talk to other nurses and physicians in English about patients and to read patient histories. In some cases, they also needed to be able to talk to patients and their families in English. The provider needed to determine which of the designated nurses already possessed the requisite English skills and which needed English language training. For the latter group, the provider also needed to ascertain whether differences in proficiency levels would warrant separate class groupings. Because assessment would be conducted by an ESOL professional rather than a medical professional, assessment tasks had to be accessible to a lay reader.

For the assessment instrument, the trainer developed a simple integrated skills task that involved retelling a story. Relatively short narrative cases were taken from technically accurate medical materials written for access by lay persons. Each potential participant was given a fixed time to read the cases and process the content. Then the potential participant returned the case to the examiner and retold the case orally. The retelling was audiotaped.

Two forms of assessment were used. While listening to the retelling, the examiner rated it for overall intelligibility on a 5-point scale with simple descriptors, with 5 being the highest. The second evaluation involved recall of idea units. Each case had been analyzed for the number of idea units, which were listed on a form. Listening to each potential participant's audiotape, the examiner checked off the idea units on the form.

The provider administered this test to several nurses whose English the hospital administrators considered satisfactorily fluent. This established the descriptors for Level 5 on the overall intelligibility rating scale and the number of idea units that made up a score of "complete" on the idea unit scale. The provider was then able to develop descriptors for the other levels on the two scales and to assess each potential participant's performance on the assessment task using these scores.

The production of a written report also has advantages for the workplace language training provider. By laying out the data in an organized manner and tracing connections and relationships among various categories of information, the provider becomes better able to see the areas of greatest need and more fully equipped to make clear recommendations regarding the potential training participants and the content and priorities of the instructional program.

In the written report, the workplace language training provider relates identified needs to the originally stated goals of the program and suggests ways of setting priorities for topics and skills. The report gives the provider an opportunity to help the client articulate communication needs more clearly, recognize the ways in which skills are related and build on one another, and understand what can and cannot be accomplished in a given period of training.

Case Study 5.5: Assessment Report for Corporation Recommends Variation of Initial Program Focus

A U.S. corporation asked a communication skills training firm to provide English language training for employees in its technical support division. The employees in question came from a variety of Asian and Eastern European backgrounds. During the organizational needs assessment, the human resources director and several company managers stated that these technicians needed a program that would improve their English speaking skills. They need to be able to provide technical support to customers on the phone as well as internal support to other employees who were experiencing problems with their equipment.

The instructional needs assessment confirmed the need for a focus on speaking skills related to their job tasks. The workplace language training provider reviewed customer comment cards, interviewed the technicians' internal customers (other employees), and conducted assessment interviews with the technicians themselves in which they encouraged the technicians to express their needs and wishes for English language training. In all cases, speaking skills were identified as paramount in importance.

When writing the formal report on the results of the instructional needs assessment, however, the provider reviewed the interview notes, audiotaped oral assessments again, and recognized another major need. In many cases, confusion arose for internal and external customers because the technician was not answering the question the customer had asked or not addressing the point the customer had raised. Customers had difficulty understanding the technicians not only because the technicians did not have strong speaking skills but also because the technicians were not providing the expected responses. The issue in these cases was not the technicians' speaking skills, but their listening comprehension and use of strategies for ensuring that they had understood the customers' questions.

As a result, in the report the training provider recommended that instruction focus at first on targeted listening practice and applying strategies for ensuring that the question the technician heard was the question the customer had asked. The resulting program was highly successful, with a dramatic increase in external and internal customer satisfaction ratings within 6 months after it began.

Conclusion

The instructional needs assessment is the basis for a successful workplace language training program. Because it identifies the present situation (PSA) of participants and the target situation (TSA), it demarcates clear starting and ending points for the workplace language training program. It thus lays the foundation for targeted instruction, ongoing assessment of participant progress, and achievement of program goals. It ensures that the provider will develop an instructional program that is relevant to participants' workplace communication needs and that will enable participants to transfer the skills they learn in class to the workplace.

Effective Practice **6**

The Workplace Language Training Provider Creates a Flexible, Research-Based Instructional Design

Overview

To create an appropriate instructional design for a workplace language training program, the training provider begins with the goals outlined during the organizational needs assessment and the language training needs identified during the instructional needs assessment. The provider recasts these as initial performance objectives: what program participants will know and be able to do as a result of the training. In a language training program, what participants will know is the set of specific language skills that they will possess; what they will be able to do is the set of specific communication functions and tasks, such as offering assistance, giving instructions, or writing short informational memos, that they will be able to carry out.

The workplace language training provider then uses communication task/language analysis (CT/LA) to identify the linguistic components that must be taught in order to enable participants to accomplish each task. Linguistic components include grammatical structures, vocabulary, sentence structure, vocal inflection (for oral communication tasks), exchange patterns (for oral interaction), and paragraph and longer text structure (for written communication).

Having carried out the CT/LA, the provider creates a sequence for teaching the various communication tasks. The sequence is informed by the provider's knowledge of effective teaching methodology and the relative urgency or priority that has been assigned to different tasks by the client. The provider seeks to create a sequence that will enable participants to build on previously acquired knowledge, allow opportunities for repetition and reinforcement of key material, and be flexible enough to accommodate participants' scheduling needs and to permit adjustment as instructional needs change or are clarified.

The product of the instructional design process is a written course outline or syllabus that defines the program's performance objectives and shows the client and the participants how the workplace language training provider intends to accomplish them. For effective workplace language training providers, instructional design involves five practices.

Practice 6.1: translate program goals and instructional needs assessment into initial performance objectives

Practice 6.2: conduct a communication task/language analysis for each task or topic area listed in the performance objectives

Practice 6.3: on the basis of principles of language learning and client priorities, develop an appropriate framework for sequencing topics and tasks

Practice 6.4: create an instructional schedule that accommodates participant and client needs

Practice 6.5: produce a written course document that allows for adjustment when necessary

Practice 6.1: Translate Program Goals and Instructional Needs Assessment Into Initial Performance Objectives

The first step in the creation of an instructional design for a workplace language training program is one of translation. The training provider lists the goals outlined during the organizational needs assessment and the needs identified during the instructional needs assessment, and then recasts them as a series of initial performance objectives. Each performance objective describes something that program participants will know or be able to do with language as a result of the training. Among some training providers, these are called *SKAs* (skills, knowledge, and abilities), and performance objectives are referred to as *learner outcomes.*

Outlining the performance objectives for participants in a training program is a straightforward process when the organizational and instructional needs assessments have been carried out thoroughly. By showing the language training provider what participants need to know and be able to do, what level of training effort the client is able to support, and what participants' current proficiency levels are, the assessments supply all of the information the provider needs to develop realistic, achievable learner outcomes.

The definition of a performance objective has three parts.

1. the specific communication function, such as giving instructions or taking a phone message

2. the task: the function and the conditions under which it is performed

3. the criteria for acceptable performance (communicative competence): accuracy of language use, politeness, number of clarifications needed

Performance objectives are forward looking. They are not simple statements of classroom activities, but measurable outcomes that a learner is expected to reach by the end of a certain period of training. For this reason, objectives are defined in specific terms; if they are vague, neither the participants nor the training provider will know when the desired level of knowledge has been achieved.

Because they are specific and measurable, performance objectives allow the workplace language training provider, the client, and the program participants to document progress while a training program is taking place. Performance objectives also provide the basis for a major segment of the evaluation of the program after its completion.

Case Study 6.1: Financial Services Firm Works With Provider to Create Performance Objectives

A large financial services institution in the United States employed a number of nonnative speakers of English as service representatives. The majority of the customer interactions in which these representatives participated were telephone conversations with bank officers located all over the country. Recognizing that communication between the representatives and their customers was not always satisfactory, the financial services institution asked a local language training firm to provide a program in oral communication skills.

During the organizational needs assessment, the client told the provider that much of the interaction between representatives and customers pertained to standardized forms. In some cases, customers called in form requests and representatives sent the wrong forms. In other cases, customers provided information, and the representatives entered it incorrectly, or customers requested assistance, and representatives provided misleading or incorrect information. In addition, some customers had complained that representatives were difficult to understand and sometimes seemed brusque or standoffish.

Observing and talking with the representatives during the instructional needs assessment, the provider noted that they all had well-developed vocabularies and an excellent command of English grammar and usage. The major difficulty with their oral communication lay in two areas. They did not have a good command of the conventions of polite business conversation, and they had difficulty with intonation: the use of stress patterns and rising and falling tones. They could compensate for these deficiencies through the use of gestures and facial expressions in face-to-face communication, but not on the telephone. In phone conversations, the representatives needed to be able to use stress and intonation to distinguish questions from statements, emphasize points of significance, and convey a friendly attitude, as well as to recognize these uses of stress and intonation in the conversation of others. They also needed to have a better sense of the patterns of interaction expected in polite business conversation.

On the basis of this information, the provider developed four performance objectives for the training program.

1. Communication task: understand and respond to customer request for a form
      Conditions: customer calls to request form; representative must determine which form is needed
      Criteria for acceptable performance:
      • representative is able to understand customer with minimal (one or two) requests for repetition
      • representative sends the appropriate form (determined when form is returned)
      • customer feels comfortable interacting with representative (determined by established customer feedback process)

2. Communication task: answer customer questions about completing forms (give instructions)
      Conditions: customer does not understand what information is required or how to complete a section of the form and calls to request assistance
      Criteria for acceptable performance:
      • representative is able to understand customer's questions and provide appropriate responses with minimal (one or two) requests for repetition on either side

continued on page 62

continued from page 61

   - customer completes form correctly (determined when form is received)
   - customer feels comfortable interacting with representative (determined by established customer feedback process)

3. Communication task: complete form using information provided by the customer
   Conditions: customer has sent in an incomplete form; representative calls to obtain missing information
   Criteria for acceptable performance:
   - representative is able to understand customer with minimal requests for repetition
   - representative completes form correctly (determined when customer reviews form)
   - customer feels comfortable interacting with representative (determined by established customer feedback process)

4. Communication task: open and close telephone interaction with customers appropriately
   Conditions: customer calls or is called by representative
   Criteria for acceptable performance:
   - representative has repertoire of greetings and conversation openers and closings and can use them appropriately
   - customer feels comfortable interacting with representative

The provider shared these performance objectives with program participants at the beginning of the program. The participants responded positively to the objectives, noting that they gave them ways to evaluate their communication with their customers and monitor their own progress in improving their language skills. The client organization also appreciated having objectives that provided tangible ways of documenting participant progress.

Practice 6.2: Conduct a Communication Task/Language Analysis for Each Task or Topic Area Listed in the Performance Objectives

For each communication task described in the performance objectives, the workplace language training provider conducts a communication task/language analysis (CT/LA) that identifies the components that define communicative competence for that task. The provider identifies the linguistic, sociolinguistic, discourse, and strategic skills and knowledge that a program participant must possess in order to meet the criteria for acceptable performance associated with the task.

The workplace language training provider will have carried out much of the work that underlies the CT/LA process during the instructional needs assessment. In developing the program curriculum, the provider uses and expands on that work to create a comprehensive outline of the topics and tasks that it will address. The CT/LA allows the provider to identify and take advantage of connections among topics and tasks and to sequence them effectively.

The CT/LA also enables the workplace language training provider to plan for an ongoing process of learner assessment. A provider that has identified the language components that make up competence for a specific communication task will know when and how a learner can demonstrate the ability to perform that communication task in a measurable or observable way.

Case Study 6.2: Southeast Asian Hotel Asks Provider to Conduct CT/LA for Handling Complaints

The hospitality industry in a Southeast Asian country was anticipating an influx of international tourists coming to attend the Pan Pacific Games. Wanting to capitalize on this business opportunity, a hotel requested an English training program for its front desk staff. The needs assessment indicated that one primary communication task for front desk personnel was handling complaints. There were two main sources of complaints in the hotel: facilities complaints, including problems with guest rooms or noise; and service complaints, such as having to wait for service, experiencing problems with billing, or not receiving a response to inquiries. Hotel management wanted to improve the response by the front desk staff to complaints because it believed that complaints were actually opportunities for the hotel to increase guest satisfaction and build repeat business.

To assist in conducting a CT/LA for this critical job task, the workplace language training provider turned to a video-based program used internationally by the hospitality industry to train front desk personnel in handling complaints. By analyzing the authentic language in the realistic situations presented on the videotape, which also reflected the types of complaints experienced by the hotel, the provider gained an initial understanding of the key functions, grammatical structures, vocabulary, stress and intonation patterns, and nonverbal communication necessary to achieve communicative competence in the complaint management task.

The provider compared the resulting framework to observations and information gained from hotel management and employees and adjusted it according to local context (see chart below). Much of the vocabulary to be included in the instructional design was in fact predictable from the nature of complaints within any hotel, though specific relevant vocabulary depended on the features of the local hotel property.

Communication Task/Language Analysis: Handling Complaints

Functions	Language Samples	Grammar	Vocabulary	Paralanguage	Nonverbals
Listen actively	*Uh-huh.* Yes. I see. *Right.*	First person present tense	*Understand, see, right, sir/madam*	rising/falling intonation, vocalizations	eye contact, nodding, no interruptions
Ask for clarification/ confirmation	*Do you mean …? Did you say …?*	Questions, verb tenses, noun clauses	Words expressing damage, unclean conditions, poor service	rising intonation	eye contact, nodding
Apologize	*I'm so sorry. I do apologize. I regret that….*	First person, verb tenses, emphatic *do*, noun clauses	*I* (rather than *we*), *sorry, apologize, regret*	falling intonation	eye contact

continued on page 64

continued from page 63

Communication Task/Language Analysis: Handling Complaints

Functions	Language Samples	Grammar	Vocabulary	Paralanguage	Nonverbals
Promise action to be taken	*I'll have (it sent up) right away.* *I'll take care of it.*	future tenses, causative verbs	*right away, immediately, replace, check on, change, take care of, attend to*	falling intonation	eye contact, nodding
Promise to do better	*I promise this won't happen again. I can assure you that...*	present/ future tenses, noun clauses	*promise, assure, guarantee*	falling intonation	eye contact
Follow up	*Is everything all right now? Is your ... satisfactory?*	questions	*all right, satisfactory, acceptable*	rising intonation	eye contact

Practice 6.3: On the Basis of Principles of Language Learning and Client Priorities, Develop an Appropriate Framework for Sequencing Topics and Tasks

The workplace language training provider can draw on various types of organizing frameworks when determining the order of topics and tasks in the instructional design. Fundamental guidance for this process comes from two theoretical areas:

1. principles of adult learning, which illuminate adults' motivation to learn, their learning styles, and successful learning strategies

2. principles of language learning, which inform the provider's understanding of the ways in which language skills underlie and build on one another

Using these principles as a base, the provider builds the instructional framework along one or more specific dimensions: criticality, complexity, talk type, broadening responsibility, or degree of specificity to the workplace. The language training provider selects the dimension or combination of dimensions that best suits the training objectives, the learning tasks, and the learners.

The Dimension of Criticality: Urgency and Frequency

The determining factor guiding the sequencing of performance objectives in instructional design may be the client's sense of urgency. Which topics are critical due to issues of safety or accountability in the work context? How soon must program participants be able to perform the communication tasks? Urgency may also arise due to upcoming events that require participation by the learners, such as conferences, meetings, or visits by international visitors.

Specific issues that may arise in a discussion of the relative urgency of various topics and tasks include

- safety: the need to understand and communicate safety warnings and procedures in order to avoid human injury or loss of life

- regulatory agency requirements: the need to understand and communicate specific information in order to comply with laws and regulations

- customer relations: the need to communicate effectively in order to generate new business and achieve the desired level of customer satisfaction

- productivity: the need to understand and communicate instructions for the use, maintenance, and repair of material and equipment

- benefits: the need to understand and communicate work-related benefits, such as insurance coverage

The workplace language training provider also considers how frequently learners must perform specific communication tasks. Tasks that are performed more frequently have relatively greater priority in the overall curriculum framework, unless one or more of the less frequently performed tasks is considered more urgent for one of the reasons outlined above.

The Dimension of Complexity: Simple to Complex

When designing an instructional framework, workplace language training providers often start with tasks that are simple in nature and then build to those that are more complex. In such a framework, routine tasks such as greeting customers and giving instructions to coworkers precede more complex tasks such as handling complaints or participating in meetings.

The Dimension of Talk Type

When a workplace language training program focuses exclusively on oral communication skills, tasks and topics can be organized according to a framework of four *talk types*. A talk type is defined by who is talking to whom about what.

task talk: language used to carry out work tasks, such as giving directions or making requests, for example, *Reset the dial to zero; Hand me the pliers; We're almost out of paper. Place an order with the supplier.* At more complex levels, task talk includes the language used when working on teams and attending meetings.

work talk: language used to talk about work with coworkers. It is often used to build relationships and create bonds among coworkers. It is frequently negative, involving complaints about work load, supervisors, or specific tasks.

organization talk: language used for effective functioning in the broader workplace context, such as exchanging information about personnel policies, benefits, and employee rights and problems. It can also include aspects of corporate or organizational culture, that is, the often unwritten codes related to performance evaluation, raises, and advancement.

rapport talk: language used for social purposes and building relationships, such as inviting someone to go to lunch, talking about weekend activities, and asking about family.

The Dimension of Broadening Responsibility

The language of work tasks can also be organized along a continuum that progresses from current to future responsibilities for the worker. This is appropriate when workers need to master language skills not only for their current positions but also for positions to which they may be moved or promoted.

The Dimension of Degree of Specificity to the Workplace

When learners have personal learning objectives and needs in addition to those directly related to the workplace, these can be incorporated into the curriculum framework as supplementary topics. Often this provides an opportunity to help learners make connections between the ways they use English on the job and the ways they use it outside of the workplace.

Effective workplace language training providers develop curriculum frameworks in which the sequence of topics and tasks is logical to the client and the program participants because its priorities coincide with theirs. At the same time, the sequence is grounded in the provider's knowledge of the process of language skills development; the progression of topics and tasks allows participants to build on previous learning as they gain new knowledge. Finally, the framework is flexible; the sequence can be adjusted after instruction has begun to respond to emerging and previously unidentified needs.

Case Study 6.3: Provider Creates Instructional Framework for Employees of Fabric Store

A workplace language training provider was hired by a large specialty fabric store. The store asked the provider to design a program of oral ESL skills development for its sales personnel. These workers, who came from a number of Southeast Asian, Middle Eastern, and Central American countries, needed to be able to interact more effectively with store customers.

The store was divided into several departments: patterns, notions, buttons and trim, and several different fabric departments. Before the training program began, each of the participants had worked in only one department. Store management wanted all of its sales personnel to be comfortable working in every department so that they could be moved out of their regular areas when vacations or illness affected staffing levels.

During the needs assessment, the workplace language training provider identified a number of communication tasks that sales personnel needed to be able to carry out, including offering assistance; advising on colors, amounts, and styles; ringing up sales; handling merchandise returns and complaints; and taking orders for merchandise not in stock. The provider also collected lists of vocabulary items from each of the store's departments.

The instructional framework that the provider devised used a sequence that moved from department to department, week by week. Participants practiced the same set of pivotal communication tasks, gradually increasing their level of complexity as they became familiar with the vocabulary and customer needs characteristic of each department. By the end of the 12-week training program, each participant had a basic working knowledge of every one of the store's departments.

Practice 6.4: Create an Instructional Schedule That Accommodates Participant and Client Needs

In conjunction with the development of the instructional framework, the workplace language training provider develops an instructional schedule. The provider seeks to accommodate client and participant scheduling needs while developing a training time frame that will maximize participant learning.

Experience with adult learning and training shows that, particularly for low-level learners, a structure of two or three short training sessions per week spread over a period of weeks promotes learning and retention more effectively than intense full-day sessions. The expanded structure gives participants opportunities to absorb what they have learned and practice it in the workplace between sessions. As a result, participants retain more new knowledge than their counterparts in intensive training and are better able to connect it with prior knowledge and material subsequently learned.

However, the training schedule must be responsive to participants' ability to attend. In situations where the demands of work make it difficult for participants to leave work routinely two or more times a week for several weeks, a more intensive half-day or full-day schedule may be required. Similarly, if participants need to acquire English language skills quickly in order to meet an impending deadline, such as an international visit, intensive training may be the answer.

Where training is to take place over a period of weeks, the workplace language training provider must accommodate vacation and holiday schedules. This means designing instructional frameworks that provide natural stopping points where holidays or other breaks are expected.

Learners' work schedules may also require the workplace language training provider to think creatively about the ways in which training topics connect from session to session. Complicated or changing work schedules may dictate a modular structure that can be based around workplace themes or tasks, rather than a strictly sequential presentation of units.

Effective workplace language training providers have a repertoire of strategies for accommodating participant and client scheduling constraints while making the most of learning opportunities.

Case Study 6.4: Provider Creates Modular Program to Accommodate Employee Shift System of South American Oil Company

A South American oil company wanted to offer English language training at two of its oil fields. All employees in the fields worked on a shift system, but the shifts varied for different employee levels. Senior personnel worked on a system of 7 days on, 7 days off; midlevel personnel worked on a system of 11 days on, 10 days off; and low-level personnel worked on a system of 14 days on, 14 days off.

The workplace language training provider retained to design and conduct the program realized that it would be forced to offer a modular course based on multiples of seven. Each individual unit within the module would have to stand alone, not depending on any previous unit, because participants would be attending them in different sequences, depending on when they were in the field.

The provider designed a system based on a seven-unit module offered over a 28-day period. The seven 2-hour units were designed around key communication tasks; in each unit, participants worked on the linguistic, sociolinguistic, discourse, and strategic competencies associated with that particular task. Employees attended when they were in the field. At the end of 28 days, every employee had had the opportunity to attend all seven units of the module, though not in the same order or at the same time.

The provider outlined a series of these seven-unit modules, with units that repeated and reinforced key material while increasing the complexity of the language skills presented and practiced. Although no one unit could depend on any other within a given module, the modules themselves could build on one another because, at the start of each, all participants had completed all seven units of the previous one. The modular system thus gave the provider a way to increase participants' language skills while accommodating a rather challenging scheduling situation.

Practice 6.5: Produce a Written Course Document That Allows for Adjustment When Necessary

The workplace language training provider produces an instructional design/curriculum document that outlines course objectives, content, and methodology. As a written reference for all stakeholders to use, this document can avert misunderstandings and delays that may result from repeat discussions of matters that have already been resolved.

This outline of the program must remain flexible, however, because participant and client needs can change over time and because some curriculum components may require modification. As the training program unfolds, new information may become available to the workplace language training provider, including details about the specific work situations and job tasks of the participants, their learning preferences and motivations, and their attitudes toward learning. Such new information may suggest or dictate changes in the content or the sequence of instructional topics. Additional objectives may need to be integrated into the original course framework, while others may need to be dropped.

An effective instructional design/curriculum in a workplace language training program is dynamic and able to respond to new variables as they appear. When the workplace language training provider has conducted a thorough organizational and instructional needs assessment and developed a communication task-based instructional framework, the need for such adjustments is minimized, and changes are relatively easy to accommodate.

Case Study 6.5: Program for Fabric Store Employees Builds Flexibility Into Curriculum

The workplace language training provider that designed the program for the specialty fabric store described in Case Study 6.3 developed a curriculum that covered all of the store's departments, rotating from week to week. In fact, the training program was 12 weeks long, and there were only eight departments in the store. The provider's curriculum therefore allowed 2 weeks for departments that were larger or required attention to a larger number of vocabulary items and communication tasks.

This structure gave the provider the flexibility to devote more time to topics that warranted extra attention, to move ahead when participants were ready to do so, and to incorporate new topics that arose as the program progressed. A comparison of the planned curriculum and the actual sequence of training topics showed that the group had covered all of the projected material. However, the group had spent 2 weeks on one department in order to practice dealing with customer complaints. They had incorporated the subject of repairs to damaged clothing, which had not surfaced in the instructional needs assessment but which arose in the store one day. Finally, the instructor had altered the sequence of departments when a logical connection between two of them became clear.

The flexibility built into this curriculum design enabled the instructor to modify it to serve the needs of program participants as effectively as possible.

▌ Conclusion

By outlining the performance objectives and criteria for successful communication that apply to participants in a workplace language training program, the instructional design provides a road map for instruction. It shows the instructor and the participants where they are and where they need to go. The means of getting from the first point to the second is the instructional materials and activities that the workplace language training provider develops and selects. These are described in Effective Practice 7.

Effective Practice 7

The Workplace Language Training Provider Develops and Selects Program-Specific Training Materials and Activities

▤ Overview

Effective support for a workplace language training curriculum comes from the materials and activities that the workplace language training provider uses to implement it. To ensure that learning and transfer take place, these materials and activities must be authentic to the workplace. That is, they must reflect the language tasks and functions that participants are expected to use on the job and promote the development of the language skills that underlie those tasks and functions.

In effective workplace language training, instructional materials are based on materials drawn from the workplace, whether print materials that participants must read and write, or oral interactions typical of those that participants engage in on the job. Starting from these client-specific materials, the provider augments with existing materials, either the provider's own or off-the-shelf materials, that promote development of the language skills and knowledge that participants need to function effectively in the workplace.

Class activities are also based on the activities that participants engage in during the work day. Activities such as practice dialogues, role plays, and group work give participants practice in the use of language and build their confidence in their ability to use English on the job. If the work situation calls for it, these activities can also promote the development of culturally appropriate workplace skills and attitudes—the interpersonal and personal characteristics that employers expect.

Use of authentic materials and appropriate relevant activities is fundamental to ensuring that program participants are able to transfer the skills they learn in the training session to actual situations they encounter in the workplace. Such transfer must take place in order for training to accomplish its goals and have a recognizable impact in the workplace.

In developing instructional materials and activities, effective workplace language training providers engage in five practices.

Practice 7.1: develop program-specific materials from those found in the workplace

Practice 7.2: augment developed materials with appropriate existing materials

Practice 7.3: plan activities that engage learners in the authentic practice of work-related language use

Practice 7.4: plan activities that engage learners in the authentic practice of work-related skills and attitudes

Practice 7.5: plan for the appropriate use of available technology

Practice 7.1: Develop Program-Specific Materials From Those Found in the Workplace

To implement the instructional design, the workplace language training provider develops instructional materials that correlate with each of the topic areas outlined in it. The written materials and observations that the workplace language training provider has gathered during the instructional needs assessment become the foundation for these instructional materials. Among language trainers, such materials are considered authentic because they are relevant to the real-life needs of the learners. The use of such materials helps participants understand the importance of language training for their success on the job and transfer the knowledge they gain in the classroom to the workplace. Participants' confidence and motivation increase as they are able to put the skills and knowledge gained in the training sessions into practice in real work situations.

When needs assessment shows that participants need to read instructions, labels, manuals, and other print materials, an effective language training provider makes use of authentic workplace documents to teach these skills. Similarly, writing tasks that participants need to do on the job become the basis for writing practice and development of vocabulary, grammar, and language structure skills. The workplace language training provider generates exercises and learning activities that build the skills and knowledge needed for successful completion of work-related reading and writing tasks.

Work-related oral interactions provide the basis for speaking and pronunciation practice, model dialogues, and role plays. Again, the workplace language training provider generates listening and speaking practice exercises that build essential work-related oral communication skills.

The results of the instructional needs assessment are crucial to the ability of the workplace language training provider to adapt and incorporate workplace materials effectively. The information that the provider has collected on language use in the workplace provides the foundation for the materials development process, and the data collected on potential participants' language proficiency levels ensures that the developed materials will be appropriate pedagogically and culturally.

Case Study 7.1: Provider Uses Sample Currency Exchange Calls to Create Authentic Materials for Traders in Southeast Asian Bank

Before the days of the Internet, currency traders for a large national bank in Southeast Asia traded internationally by phone. English was the language of communication; traders needed to be able to understand accurately and pronounce clearly the names of currencies, buying and selling rates, and purchase statements. The bank asked a workplace language training provider to develop an English course for traders as part of a larger bank training program.

The provider recorded a sampling of currency exchange calls made by experienced traders at the bank. These recordings were used as authentic instructional materials in several ways.

First, program participants listened to the calls and analyzed them for the types and sequence of *moves* (i.e., discourse structure) made in each exchange. Through this process, participants identified the dialogue patterns that were typical of these rapid currency exchange calls. Recognition of these patterns gave participants a foundation for increasing their facility in handling such calls.

Once the relevant language patterns had been identified in the authentic recordings, the focus shifted to building accuracy and fluency in listening and speaking. The provider used the recordings for listening practice, augmenting them with recorded radio and television financial news broadcasts in which currency rates were given. These news recordings provided variety in practice, yet remained relevant to participants' work.

For the televised financial news, the picture was initially covered up so the traders would not depend on printed text. Learners wrote down each of the currencies and rates they heard. Then the screen cover was removed so they could check their comprehension. Follow-up tasks were done with transcripts of these recordings. The traders were also assigned to listen to the morning or evening financial news and exchange information in the next class session.

To develop speaking skills, program participants first transcribed the recorded telephone exchanges and used them for dialogue practice. Later, they used their analysis of the dialogue patterns to create templates for practicing new currency exchange calls.

These assignments focused on building listening and speaking fluency in the topic areas that were crucial for program participants' success in the workplace. The development of templates gave participants a technique for managing other types of interchanges, and the use of the currency news in English gave them a strategy they could use to continue building their skills beyond the class.

Practice 7.2: Augment Developed Materials With Appropriate Existing Materials

In conjunction with the development of instructional materials from authentic workplace documents and interactions, the workplace language training provider identifies existing materials that will promote the development of needed language skills and the achievement of program goals. Pre-existing materials are, by their nature, too generic to form the basis for an instructional

Case Study 7.2: Provider Customizes and Supplements Materials for Fabric Store Employees

For the fabric store described in Case Study 6.3, for which the workplace language training provider was asked to provide an English program that would enable participants to interact effectively with store customers in the various store departments, the provider started with authentic materials that included observed customer-salesperson interactions and a collection of items (e.g., fabric, buttons, trim, patterns, thread, scissors, and so on) from the store. On the basis of the instructional needs analysis, the provider knew that program participants needed to be able to ask and answer questions, describe similarities and differences, and make suggestions.

The provider had a proprietary series of exercises on *wh-* questions, *do/did* questions, comparatives and superlatives, and other relevant grammar topics. These were adapted using vocabulary from different store departments so that participants would receive repeated practice in the same grammar forms while broadening their vocabulary. The provider made similar adaptations to a set of model dialogues for customer service. Partway through the program, when participants had seen how the materials adaptation process worked, the provider encouraged them to begin creating their own exercises and model dialogues, using vocabulary they wanted or needed to practice.

The provider also recommended the use of a well-known picture dictionary, which the client provided for each participant. The picture dictionary contained many items relevant to the learners' work setting, and the provider encouraged participants to use it to explore new vocabulary as they did exercises and created model dialogues.

The picture dictionary also answered another need. Participants understood that the purpose of the program was to help them improve their work-related English language skills. However, a number of them were interested in improving their general communication skills as well. The picture dictionary gave them a tool to use for this purpose, enhancing their already positive perceptions of the training program.

curriculum that is tailored to client needs and circumstances. However, they can be useful as supplements that provide practice in specific skills or topic areas.

In some cases, the provider may have proprietary materials that it has developed itself for use in previous language training programs and can adapt for use with the current participant population. Such materials may include oral language exercises that target common pronunciation and intonation challenges as well as reading and writing tasks that reinforce points of grammar and sentence structure. They may also include task-specific materials, such as guidelines for making polite requests or vocabulary for giving directions to specific locations.

In other cases, the provider may recommend an off-the-shelf textbook or workbook for use as an instructional supplement. Publishers of instructional materials for adult ESL learners have developed a number of textbooks that address specific communication topics, such as telephone techniques and business writing, and specific types of work, such as medical English, legal English, English for finance, and English for technology fields. In some cases, these may be adaptable for specific groups. In other cases, they may be too general. In addition, publishers offer a number of picture dictionaries, idiom dictionaries, pronunciation guides, and grammar guides.

An effective workplace language training provider can identify proprietary and off-the-shelf materials that are appropriate to the nature of the training program and the proficiency levels of participants. The provider integrates these with the materials developed from workplace documents and interactions to create a cohesive, sequenced set of instructional materials that builds skills and promotes transfer.

Practice 7.3: Plan Activities That Engage Learners in the Authentic Practice of Work-Related Language Use

In addition to using authentic workplace materials, an effective workplace language trainer uses learner-centered instruction to engage participants in authentic activities. Such activities mimic those in which participants engage on the job, allowing them to practice work-related tasks and gain confidence in their ability to carry them out successfully.

Practice dialogues derived from authentic workplace interactions, such as those described above, form the first level of such practice activities for oral communication. However, in real situations, oral interaction rarely follows a script. To prepare learners for actual work-related interactions, the workplace language training provider helps them move beyond scripted language through a series of progressively less-structured role plays. Role playing gives participants opportunities to apply their new language skills in a supportive context, discovering for themselves what works and what does not.

A key aspect of such practice is that it enables learners to recognize miscommunication and develop strategies for managing it when it occurs. The workplace language training provider introduces strategies for ensuring that one has understood another speaker, language for requesting clarification, and polite ways of correcting a misunderstanding on the part of another person. By using these techniques in classroom role plays, and later by using them in workplace situations and reporting back on their success, participants develop confidence in their ability to use language effectively and motivation to take responsibility for their own learning.

For programs focusing on writing and reading tasks, authentic practice is equally important. As with oral communication, writing and reading practice begin with the identification of typical patterns and the imitation of models, moving over time to writing tasks that incorporate less formal guidance. The practice writing tasks are based on those that participants must do at work: letters, instructions, reports, and so on. Participants work in pairs or small groups to review one another's writing, as they would in the workplace, where reports and longer documents are often produced by a team.

Workplace language training providers also give program participants opportunities to practice the use of work-related language through job tasks identified in the needs assessment, which may include description of what they do and how they do it. These activities often involve the use or creation of visual aids that support the development of a common understanding. Participants may use pictures of equipment, or the actual equipment if it is available, as they describe how it is used. They may draw diagrams and floor plans to illustrate procedures and systems, or create time lines to illustrate a sequence of steps. They may also create instructions or guidelines for themselves and their coworkers, or visual materials such as safety posters for the work site.

Case Study 7.3: Community-Based Organization Ensures That Classes for Garment Workers Offer Authentic, Work-Related Language Practice

A community-based organization (CBO) developed workplace English classes for garment workers in New York City's Chinatown. First-line supervisors in the garment industry in New York's Chinatown are usually bilingual, so entry-level garment workers can perform their jobs satisfactorily without English. However, English proficiency is the main criterion upon which advancement to better positions is based. The classes at the CBO were designed for entry-level piece workers and focused on basic workplace terminology, safety, and job-related interpersonal communication.

The CBO learned from program participants that effective oral communication on the job was their greatest weakness as well as the most critical key to advancement on the job. The trainer and curriculum developer therefore built into the curriculum a series of common workplace situations in which piece workers might have to communicate in English with others—for example, explaining to a trucker where to pick up waiting merchandise, conveying concerns about a potential part-time lay-off to a supervisor or human resources personnel, or conveying critical information for the staff on the next shift. Activities based on these situations began with structured practice dialogues and moved participants gradually to more free-form role plays as their confidence increased.

The trainer used materials from the workplace as visual aids while introducing the English terms for various parts of garments (e.g., *shoulder pad, collar, sleeve, yoke, dart, cuff, gather*). Participants practiced the use of a select number of related vocabulary items each week, ending with a quiz. For example, in the week in which they learned terms for *collars* and *necklines*, the quiz involved drawing and labeling five kinds of collars and five kinds of necklines.

In one training session, the topic was quality control and garment defects. The language trainer distributed a handout and listed various types of defects on the board. He showed actual samples and asked students if defects were present in *hems* (e.g., *wavy, visible on outside*), *belt loops* (e.g., *crooked, missing, too small*), *zippers* (e.g., *defective operation, visible when closed*), and other areas. He then reviewed the language associated with garment defects, using samples, explanations, descriptions, and translation. In an amusing moment, he put his own sports coat on, expecting no defects, and invited the participants to find defects. He was surprised by the number of defects they found on his coat.

Practice 7.4: Plan Activities That Engage Learners in the Authentic Practice of Work-Related Skills and Attitudes

In addition to expecting or desiring a certain level of language proficiency, every employer has expectations for employee behavior and characteristics. These expectations are based on the culturally conditioned definitions of the skills and attitudes of a so-called *good* employee or business person, and have to do with the ways in which an employee interacts with superiors, customers, and coworkers; responds to problems and conflicts in the workplace; and displays loyalty, motivation, respect, initiative, integrity, and other valued personal qualities.

The workplace language training provider can help program participants understand and feel comfortable with culturally conditioned behaviors through the use of activities that encourage them to practice those behaviors in the classroom. In EFL situations, where participants are learning English for international business purposes, such activities focus on cultural contrasts in the world of international business. They illustrate the characteristics and behaviors that are typical of business people from other countries and the expectations that such people have for interaction in international business settings. The focus is on qualities that are valued and the ways in which those qualities are demonstrated and interpreted. The workplace language training provider develops activities that enable participants to recognize the cultural elements of international business communication and develop a personal style that allows them to interact effectively across cultures while maintaining their own cultural integrity.

In ESL situations, where English is the language of the country in which participants live as well as of their workplace, the language training provider can teach culturally appropriate workplace behaviors through classroom activities and reinforce them through classroom management techniques. The focus is on helping participants adopt behaviors and attitudes that will enable them to demonstrate the qualities employers expect of good employees.

In the United States, workplace language training providers refer to *Equipped for the Future* (EFF) (National Institute for Literacy, n.d.), an outline of the skills that employers say workers must possess in order to succeed in the 21st-century workplace. EFF, developed by the National Institute for Literacy, describes skills in communicating, making decisions, solving problems, planning, working in teams, negotiating, resolving conflicts, and taking responsibility for learning. The characteristics that underlie many of these skills are thought of as initiative, motivation, and being a team player and are valued highly by U.S. employers. Employees who are nonnative speakers of English, however, may come from cultures in which these qualities are regarded negatively and may find it difficult to adapt to a different perception. Similar excellent work in defining workplace communication competencies has been done in other English-speaking countries.

Effective workplace language training providers respond to this need through the use of classroom management techniques that provide a supportive context in which participants can try out behaviors that are unfamiliar or alien. In that supportive context, language training providers encourage participants to work in pairs or teams, develop alternate solutions to hypothetical problems, create plans and describe how they would implement them, and contribute materials and ideas from their own work contexts to the pool of sources for instructional materials. These activities increase participants' level of comfort with the culture of the U.S. workplace, prompt participants to take responsibility for their own learning, and help them develop the skills that will contribute to their success in the workplace.

Case Study 7.4: Provider Builds Program for Airline Ground Crew Around Authentic Tasks

In a workplace English program for the employees of a major airline, the majority of the participants were ground crew. The focus of the program was oral communication with coworkers and the tower, and the relationships between oral language and the hand signals used with pilots.

The instructor created four program-related job descriptions: resource manager, attendance monitor, timekeeper, and evaluator.

- resource manager: responsible for bringing relevant work-related items and materials, such as tools and safety equipment, to class and returning them afterwards

- attendance monitor: responsible for tracking attendance of all participants and for gathering notification in advance from participants who had to miss a class session

- timekeeper: responsible for monitoring the progress of each class session against the agenda posted by the instructor at the beginning of each class to ensure that the group stayed on task

- evaluator: responsible for assessing the effectiveness of class activities and learners' participation in them to determine whether activities were effective in helping learners develop the language skills they needed on the job and whether participants were making the most of this learning opportunity

The instructor divided the 18-member class into four teams. Each team took one of the four job descriptions as its task each week so that by the end of the 8-week training program, each team had performed each job twice.

At the end of training, participants' supervisors evaluated the changes they had seen in their employees. In addition to commenting positively on improvement in employees' language skills, the supervisors noted a marked change for the better in employees' apparent motivation on the job. "Takes more initiative now," said one, and another wrote, "Has become a pleasure to work with."

Participants also provided written evaluations of the program, and many of them commented on this classroom management technique. They noted that, although they were not comfortable with it at first, it became easier as time went by and helped them learn how to work together more effectively. "This training was really for us," one wrote. "It worked because we made it work."

Practice 7.5: Plan for the Appropriate Use of Available Technology

When circumstances permit, the workplace language training provider takes advantage of technology to enhance classroom activities and participant learning. Technology can contribute in three ways: as the basis for authentic practice activities, as a support for the learning that is taking place in the classroom, and as the mechanism for distance learning.

When the communication tasks that program participants must carry out on the job involve the use of some form of technology, the provider can design instructional activities around that technology. For example, if participants are required to give instructions for the use of a specific piece of equipment, participants can practice with the actual equipment, if it is accessible, or with a photograph or drawing of it. Participants whose jobs require telephone communication can practice with real telephones, if these are available.

Technology can be a useful adjunct to classroom instruction. In programs whose focus is oral communication, audio- and videotaping are effective ways to help participants hear themselves as others hear them and identify the areas in which they need to improve pronunciation and intonation. When the focus is on writing tasks, participants and instructor can use e-mail communication for practice and feedback. Computer-based instructional programs can also be useful adjuncts to regular instruction when they address the performance objectives of the specific workplace language training program in which they are used.

Distance learning is difficult to implement successfully in workplace language training because, without a major investment of time and resources, it precludes the interaction that underlies effective language learning. When distance education is the only available option, but direct synchronic interaction through audio and video links is not available, television, radio, and the telephone all provide options. In teleteaching, for example, each learner phones the instructor at an appointed time for one-on-one teaching or teleconferencing. E-mail and audiotapes sent through the mail are other options.

Effective workplace language training providers use the technology that is available as a support for instruction rather than as its main focus. When involved in distance education, they use technology in ways that maximize interaction among participants and between participants and instructor.

Case Study 7.5: Community-Based Organization
Expands Classroom Program for Garment Workers
Into Distance Learning Program on Radio and Television

The Chinese American CBO that developed the program for garment workers described in Case Study 7.3 received funding to make its program available to garment workers in other cities across North America. The objective was to convert the training to a distance education format.

The CBO developed 100 five-minute radio broadcast segments, with two accompanying booklets and achievement tests for workers to complete and submit for evaluation. The five-minute segments were broadcast on Sinocast Radio at a designated time during the work day. The CBO also developed six garment-related units that trainees could use in a computer lab, and 27 ten-minute video episodes of garment-related language training, which were broadcast two or three times a week on SinoVision TV in the evenings.

Each video episode included a bilingual review of workplace terminology with and without visuals, the presentation of a dialogue designed to use the terminology, and a practice segment entitled "What is this?" Each computer unit included reading material with a Chinese-English glossary of terms and expressions and a self-score test. All instructions were provided in English and Chinese.

Although this distance learning program could not provide the interpersonal interaction required for major improvement of on-the-job speaking skills, its use of a variety of media did help participants improve their work-related listening comprehension and vocabulary. Data collected later from adult education programs in the cities where the program was broadcast showed that, when enrolled in regular adult ESL classes, Chinese learners who had had exposure to the program progressed faster than their counterparts who had not been exposed to it.

Conclusion

The materials and activities that the workplace language training provider develops and selects for use in a training program are the tools that make an instructional design function. When materials and activities are authentic to the workplace, they not only promote learning, they also encourage the transfer of learned skills to real-life workplace settings and situations. Effective instructional materials and activities, whether specific to the program or off the shelf, enable workplace language training providers to conduct the kind of dynamic, responsive instruction described in chapter 8 and to evaluate it as it is taking place.

Effective Practice 8

The Workplace Language Training Provider Delivers Instruction That Keeps Participants Involved and Motivated

▓ Overview

Delivering instruction is the culmination of all the preparatory work that the workplace language training provider and the client have done through needs assessment, program planning, staff recruitment, instructional curriculum design, and materials development. At this point, the workplace language training provider applies instructional strategies and approaches that will make the training program effective and rewarding for all participants, being sensitive to the motivations and attitudes that participants bring from their past educational experiences. The provider involves supervisors and other workplace staff in ways that will enhance participants' learning.

While providing instruction, the provider conducts ongoing evaluation of the curriculum to ensure that it is meeting the program's goals and modifies it if necessary. In addition, the provider reviews the program goals themselves to ensure that they are still appropriate and sufficient. The provider also monitors participant attendance and assesses participant progress in relation to the performance objectives outlined in the instructional plan.

When instruction concludes, the provider and client representatives acknowledge the work that participants have done through some form of recognition, such as a certificate.

The provision of instruction by a workplace language training provider entails five practices.

Practice 8.1: use appropriate language teaching approaches

Practice 8.2: involve workplace supervisors and other staff appropriately

Practice 8.3: conduct formative evaluation and adjust curriculum as participant or client needs become clearer or change

Practice 8.4: monitor the training and maintain communication with the client

Practice 8.5: provide recognition of completion to participants and recognition of contributions to client representatives

Practice 8.1: Use Appropriate Language Teaching Approaches

As noted in the Introduction, developments in the theory of adult learning and language acquisition have led many effective workplace language training providers to adopt an approach to instruction that is learner centered and task based. In this approach, learners participate actively in every class session, developing and practicing language skills as they work together in teams or pairs on specific communication tasks and problems. The instructor models linguistic, sociolinguistic, discourse, and strategic competence at key points, then serves as a resource for learners as they practice the language themselves. Activities include role plays, group projects, and collaborative writing, and learners contribute to the curriculum by bringing communication challenges they have encountered in the workplace to class for discussion.

Learner-centered instruction enables participants to build on the knowledge and experience they already possess and encourages them to take responsibility for their own learning. However, some adult trainees may have had unpleasant or unsuccessful schooling experiences in the past and lack the confidence to participate fully in training. Others may have been highly successful in traditional schools and be resistant to instructional methods that differ from those they know. Cultural considerations can also affect participants' ability to take advantage of learner-centered

---

Case Study 8.1: Provider Builds Student Confidence by Moving From Traditional Dialogues to Open-Ended Activities

In the program for garment workers designed by a community-based organization (CBO) (see Case Study 7.3), the focus was on effective oral communication with colleagues and supervisors. The trainer and the curriculum developer built into the curriculum a series of common workplace situations in which piece workers might have to communicate in English with others—for example, explaining to a trucker where to pick up waiting merchandise, conveying concerns about a potential part-time lay-off to a supervisor or human resources personnel, or conveying critical information for the staff on the next shift.

These situations were originally developed to be used in role-playing activities. The trainer soon found, however, that program participants were reluctant to take part in the role plays, especially to take the role of someone in a position different from their own.

Talking with participants with the assistance of an interpreter, the curriculum developer learned that all of their previous educational experiences had been highly traditional, with an emphasis on attending to the instructor and producing only correct answers. As a result, the participants were more comfortable with the use of fixed dialogues that gave them models of correct language use for practice and emulation. This was especially true for roles such as trucker and supervisor, where participants felt their experience could not help them.

The curriculum developer then created a series of dialogues for each target situation. Each series included a fixed dialogue that participants could repeat for practice, and two other dialogues that supplied two options (equivalent in meaning) for each turn in the interaction. Through the use of these dialogues, program participants became more confident in their own language ability and more comfortable with the idea of creating their own dialogues. They then moved on successfully to role-playing and simulation activities.

---

instruction. Participants whose educational backgrounds include only traditional teacher-centered instruction, in which the teacher talks and learners listen, repeat chorally, and practice individually, may be uncomfortable with an approach that encourages learners to take chances and make mistakes. In addition, where the culture of the workplace is highly bureaucratic or the sociocultural context is class conscious, when class groups consist of mixed populations, participants whose rank is relatively lower on the scale may be reluctant to work in groups or to speak in front of those whose rank is relatively higher.

Effective workplace language training providers are sensitive to such possibilities and remain alert to their emergence as participants become more comfortable expressing themselves to the trainer. They are able to employ an eclectic mixture of traditional (e.g., repetition, dialogue recitation, cognitive grammar drills) and learner-centered approaches (e.g., role plays) to meet the needs and expectations of program participants, and they maintain awareness of status and other relationships that may exist among participants when designing and implementing learning activities. When possible, they take advantage of such relationships to create activities that are authentic to the workplace.

Practice 8.2: Involve Workplace Supervisors and Other Staff Appropriately

As a general rule, workplace language training providers advise against involving supervisors and subordinates in training together. In some situations, however, involving supervisors or other staff from the workplace in other ways can be helpful. The ideal role of supervisors and other workplace staff not regularly involved with the training is to participate on an occasional basis in lifelike role plays and simulations. Such involvement serves to reinforce the customized workplace focus of the training program for participants. It also allows supervisors and others to see the training program in action, which can contribute to confidence in the program and reinforcement of a strong client-provider relationship.

Human resources managers, supervisors, and other client representatives may request opportunities to observe a class session. Such observation can affect participants' willingness to take part in instructional activities because they may fear making a mistake or expressing their opinions in the presence of someone in a higher position.

Effective workplace language training providers welcome in-class observations as opportunities to create authentic instructional activities. Explaining the effect that the presence of an observer can have on participants' behavior and learning, they request that potential observers notify them of their intention in advance so that the class can be informed that an observer will be present and participating in part of the class session. They then use the observer's presence as an occasion for authentic practice of skills relevant to participants' relationship with the observer.

Case Study 8.2: Representatives From Semiconductor Plant and Provider Work Together to Develop Program

In a U.S. plant that manufactures semiconductor components, a number of Russian refugees with advanced postgraduate engineering degrees were hired for entry-level technician positions because of their limited English proficiency. Most of the supervisors of these technicians had only secondary school levels of education and could not interpret the blueprints that came from the engineering department. The Russian technicians, on the other hand, could understand the content of the blueprints well.

In one instance when there was a rush order bound for a major client, one of the Russian technicians discovered a significant flaw in part of the blueprint. Unable to explain the problem in English or make his supervisor understand, the technician corrected the problem on the blueprint in Russian. All of his fellow technicians understood the problem and were very concerned that the correction be made. However, their supervisor would not approve the change because he could not read Russian. The order went out defective, and a major delay ensued when it had to be redone, causing the client to express dissatisfaction.

This situation motivated the plant to engage a workplace language training provider to work with its Russian technicians. Working together, the provider and plant representatives developed a plan for all pertinent parties to participate in a series of class sessions together after the Russian technicians had reached a certain level of proficiency in English. The joint sessions would give the technicians, their supervisors, and members of the engineering department an opportunity to address the problem that had occurred and develop a strategy for preventing similar miscommunications in future.

The provider met with management representatives to learn the recommended procedures for handling such a situation successfully. The provider then met with members of the engineering department and with the technicians' supervisors to explain the purpose of their participation in the training and to reduce any feelings of discomfort. Finally, the provider prepared the Russian technicians themselves for the series of classes with others present.

The curriculum for those sessions was designed on the basis of input from the Russian technicians about what they needed to know linguistically and in terms of corporate communication channels. The resulting lesson plans were shared in advance with all parties involved so that all would be fully prepared to achieve the problem-solving outcome that was needed.

As a result of this special training, the Russian technicians gained the language skills they needed, inter- and intradepartmental communication procedures were clarified, and everyone involved became confident that such situations would be handled appropriately in the future.

Practice 8.3: Conduct Formative Evaluation and Adjust Curriculum as Participant or Client Needs Become Clearer or Change

One feature that is particular to workplace language training is that the curriculum emerges as greater insight about participants' workplace needs become evident during the training. Such changes or clarified needs normally become evident through an effective, ongoing formative evaluation process.

Formative evaluation refers to evaluation that takes place as a training program is underway. It contrasts with *summative evaluation*, which takes place after a program is completed. The purpose of formative evaluation is to assess the way in which a training program is progressing in relation to its goals and also to review the goals themselves to ensure that they are still sufficient and appropriate.

Formative evaluation is based on feedback from program participants, input from supervisors and other client representatives, and the observations of the instructor. Participants report, either orally or in writing, on what they are learning and how they are using their new skills in the workplace. Supervisors and other client representatives report their observations of changes in participants' language proficiency and their ability to accomplish work-related communication

---

Case Study 8.3: Community College Program for Mexican Laborers Restructures Classes as New Needs Emerge

A local community college was asked to provide workplace English language training for immigrant Mexican laborers working in the carpet-making industry in a southern U.S. state. The immigrant workers, who had been brought into the United States by a consortium of area carpet manufacturers to offset a labor shortage, had settled in the area and, in many cases, saved enough money to send for their families to join them. With funding from the U.S. government and the manufacturers, the community college was to provide a program that would give participants the English language skills they needed to be productive in the workplace and also to function as citizens in their new community.

The community college conducted a needs assessment, developed an instructional curriculum, and began the training. Partway through the first training module, the instructor found herself staying after almost every class session to answer questions about the English language terms for various illnesses and health issues. Exploring the reasons for this with the participants, the instructor learned that many of them wanted to be able to talk about their own and their children's health with medical professionals. They had not mentioned this need during the needs assessment because they had understood that the program was about English for the workplace and for participation in matters of public life, such as voting and schools.

The instructor and the program director took this issue to the funding organizations, and together they devised a plan for restructuring the curriculum to include a unit on health-related language. The restructuring actually resulted in an improvement in the program because the instructor was able to connect the health unit with a topic already in the curriculum: safety on the job.

tasks. These short reports give program participants and client representatives opportunities to identify needs that have emerged since the initial needs assessment was done.

The observations of the instructor include notes on participants' progress as well as lesson plans with notes on which activities were most supportive of participants' language skill development and which topics or tasks require repetition or review. These notes guide the provider in formative evaluation as a program is progressing and also provide a basis for planning additional training.

Effective workplace language training providers include a plan for formative evaluation in the program outline presented in the original proposal to the client. The plan connects this ongoing evaluation with the program monitoring and client communication described in Practice 8.4.

Practice 8.4: Monitor the Training and Maintain Communication With the Client

Monitoring training means tracking participants' learning and monitoring logistical aspects of the program. This monitoring, combined with ongoing formative evaluation, enables the workplace language training provider to report to the client on a regular basis while the program is underway.

An effective workplace language training program assesses participant progress regularly during the training cycle. Assessment serves to document how well the participants are learning the English they need to perform workplace communication tasks. For this reason, assessment is customized to the program through the use of role plays and simulations that allow the participant to demonstrate ability level in relation to the performance objectives and criteria outlined in the instructional curriculum. For example, the trainer may have participants demonstrate making an appointment over the telephone.

In some cases, the client or a sponsoring organization requires the use of standardized tests for monitoring participant progress. Because they are designed for general use, such tests cannot accurately reflect participants' ability to accomplish the performance objectives of a specific workplace language training program. In such cases, an effective workplace language training provider will present data from a customized assessment together with the results of standardized testing in order to give the client an accurate picture of participants' progress.

The workplace language training provider also maintains written records of participants' attendance and of any logistical problems, such as locked rooms or missing equipment, that have a negative effect on the training program and were not addressed in the planning process.

Careful monitoring allows the provider to address problems while they are still minor and easily solved. Regular communication between provider and client is therefore an essential adjunct to monitoring. Effective workplace language training providers work with client representatives in the program development stage to outline a schedule for conducting and reporting on formative evaluation, participant assessment, and attendance and other logistical matters.

Case Study 8.4: Private Language School in Indonesia Establishes Reporting Routine With Instructors

A private language training center at a university in Jakarta, Indonesia, had a contract to provide workplace English language training for the Indonesian Ministry of Agriculture. The program took place at the Ministry's regional headquarters, located 120 miles east of Jakarta. Funding for the program came from a United Nations (U.N.) organization.

The aim of the program was to provide agricultural extension agents with the English needed to read instruction manuals for agricultural equipment, read reports and research articles in agricultural journals, handle written correspondence with agencies and individuals outside the country, handle basic social interactions with visiting international experts, and understand lectures and demonstrations given by visiting international experts.

The academic director of the language training center needed to report regularly to the Ministry and representatives of the U.N. organization on the progress of the training program. However, she was able to make only one 1-day visit per month to the training site. She therefore established a regular reporting routine with the two program instructors.

The two instructors alternated at the training site: One would spend a week on site, teaching the intensive program of 30 hours per week, while the other would spend time in Jakarta, resting and recuperating. At the end of each week, the instructor on duty would return to Jakarta, bringing attendance records to the academic director and making an oral report on learner progress, learner attitudes, meetings with the on-site training manager, requests for materials, and other needs and events.

The academic director would then make appropriate changes in the instructional curriculum and pack up training and office supplies. At the end of the week, she would meet with the instructor to review her instructions for the week. She would also give the instructor a written progress report to deliver to the on-site training manager.

This procedure enabled the academic director to remain aware of developments in the program and to remain in close contact with the on-site training manager, despite the remote location of the program and the infrequency of her site visits. By relying on the instructors to provide thorough reports every week, the academic director was able to monitor developments in the field and follow up closely on everything the instructors reported in order to be aware of what was really happening at the training site.

Practice 8.5: Provide Recognition of Completion to Participants and Recognition of Contributions to Client Representatives

Many workplaces employ specific strategies to enhance positive attitudes, loyalty, and high productivity. Workplace language training providers participate in this tradition by providing appropriate displays of recognition for completion of training. Such recognition gives participants a sense of closure at the end of the training program and a feeling of accomplishment that contributes to their self-esteem.

Recognition for program participants usually takes the form of certificates of completion, which may be given out at a graduation ceremony. In some cases, a senior manager or company executive hands out the certificates and congratulates participants personally. Some workplace language training providers give out small tokens, such as lapel pins, in recognition of participants' accomplishments. The provider or the client may take photos of these ceremonies for use in newsletters and to post on employee bulletin boards.

Effective workplace language training providers often use the graduation ceremony as a time to thank the client for the training opportunity. They may present the client representative with a small gift or certificate of appreciation for the client's role in making the training program a success.

Case Study 8.5: Recognition Ceremony for Program at Agricultural Equipment Company Encourages Future Enrollment

A manufacturer of heavy agricultural equipment initiated a pilot ESOL program for 15 workers on its shop floor. The workplace language training provider that was hired to design and conduct the program planned from the outset for a graduation ceremony at which participants in the pilot program would receive a certificate and be congratulated by the president of the company. With the date set well in advance, the president was able to agree to this request.

At the graduation ceremony, the instructor gave each participant a certificate created by the workplace language training provider. The company's human resources director gave each a lapel pin in the shape of a star, a gesture that the provider had not expected but certainly appreciated. The company president shook hands and greeted each participant by name. One of the program participants served as photographer for the event.

When the last participant shook hands with the company president, the instructor took a star pin from the human resources director. As the employees laughed and applauded, she attached it to the president's lapel and proclaimed her an honorary graduate.

A few days later, the human resources manager posted photos of the graduates, holding their certificates and shaking hands with the company president, on the bulletin board in the employee cafeteria. The photo of the instructor pinning a star on the president's lapel appeared in the company newsletter the following week. When enrollment opened for the first regular offering of the program, twice the expected number of employees called to sign up. In addition, several supervisors called the human resources director to inquire about serving as tutors for their employees. "They're great folks and I'd like to help them out," said one. "I figure if it's that important to the president, it ought to be important to me."

Conclusion

In delivering instruction, the goal of the workplace language training provider is to enable participants to increase their language proficiency and transfer the skills they have learned in the classroom to situations they encounter in the workplace. The provider's ability to accomplish this goal depends on the thoroughness of the preparatory work that has preceded instruction itself and the provider's ability to recognize emergent needs and respond to them appropriately as instruction is taking place. The formative evaluation and assessment of participant progress that the provider carries out while conducting the program guide the identification and response to such emergent needs and also provide the initial data for the final summative evaluation that will take place at the program's end.

Effective Practice 9

The Workplace Language Training Provider Conducts a Program Evaluation That Relates Program Outcomes to Program Goals and Serves as a Guide for Future Training

Overview

Evaluation of a workplace language training program provides essential information about the value of training, the aspects of the training program that were effective and can be repeated or built upon in future programs, and the aspects that need to be rethought or changed in some way. Summative evaluation, which takes place when a program has ended, is most often conducted by the workplace language training provider, although in government-funded and some other situations, another agency may be retained to evaluate the program and the training provider.

Evaluation works best when the reasons for evaluating are clearly delineated so that the provider and client know what information is being collected and why. Areas for evaluation may include participant learning, program logistics, cost effectiveness, and impact on the organization. Once the reasons for evaluating are delineated, the workplace language training provider selects an evaluation model and defines evaluation mechanisms that will allow it to obtain the desired information. An effective evaluation process often parallels the needs assessment process that took place before the program began because evaluation seeks to learn whether the goals defined at the outset have been met.

Effective workplace language training providers regard evaluation as an essential component of any training program. Through evaluation, providers solidify their trust relationships with their clients as they monitor the quality of their performance and obtain information that can guide their development.

Evaluation of a workplace language training program involves five practices.

Practice 9.1: outline the reasons for evaluating the program

Practice 9.2: identify an effective evaluation model

Practice 9.3: define and implement appropriate evaluation mechanisms

Practice 9.4: provide a written report of evaluation results and recommendations for future training

Practice 9.5: conduct periodic follow-up

Practice 9.1: Outline the Reasons for Evaluating the Program

After the workplace language training sessions have concluded, the program ends with a formal summative evaluation that assesses overall results. Such an evaluation provides essential information for all stakeholders when the client and the provider have a clear, shared understanding of what is being evaluated and why.

Participant Learning

The primary function of evaluation is often to determine what and how much program participants have learned. This type of evaluation asks

- What do participants know that they did not know before?

- What can they do that they could not do before?

- To what extent are they able to carry out the performance objectives set forth in the instructional plan?

From the client's perspective, the reasons for evaluating participant learning are threefold. Evaluation

1. shows the client the degree to which the program has met its goals

2. serves as a form of needs assessment, indicating areas where further training may be needed

3. gives the client information about the effectiveness of the workplace language training provider

From the perspective of the workplace language training provider, evaluation of participant learning provides essential information for quality control. Through evaluation of participant learning, the provider obtains feedback on which instructional designs, methods, and techniques have worked well and why, and which could be improved.

For the client and the provider, the point of evaluating participant learning is not simply to measure change, but to relate that change to the achievement of program goals and performance objectives.

Logistical Effectiveness

A second function of evaluation is to identify aspects external to the training itself that may have affected participants' ability to benefit from the training program. These aspects may include physical barriers, such as lack of adequate space, an uncomfortable training environment, or a training location that is difficult for the participants or instructor to get to. They may also include emotional factors, such as coworkers who express resentment of the training privilege or supervisors who do not help participants adjust their workload to accommodate training time, discouraging participants from attending class.

Case Study 9.1: Provider of Legal Rights Program Demonstrates Reasons to Continue Program Via Appropriate Evaluation

A U.S.-government-funded legal rights project in a Middle Eastern country included a legal and legal rights English segment. Participants in that segment were judges, prosecutors, and legal rights and community development activists.

In order to obtain continued funding for the project, the providers needed an evaluation that would demonstrate the significant positive impact of the training on participants' lives and work. For this reason, the evaluation tracked participants after the actual training had ended to determine how they were using the language skills they had learned. Several positive results were noted.

- One of the participants wrote an English-language fundraising brochure for a community development association. The brochure was successful in bringing in donations from private international sources, and those donations enabled the association to cease accepting funding from the U.S. Agency for International Development, which benefited the local reputation of the association and the U.S. budget.

- Thirty human rights and community development activists who participated in the conference presentation component of the course wrote abstracts, had papers accepted for publication, and gave presentations at local and regional human rights conferences held in English.

- Five prosecutors who began the program with intermediate-level English and completed the course were accepted in MA programs in Human Rights Law in U.S. universities. Four successfully completed their program.

Because the project providers had identified a clear purpose for evaluation, they were able to implement an evaluation process that provided solid real-world evidence of the project's success in ways that a short-term, test-oriented evaluation could not.

For client and provider, the purpose of evaluating a program's logistical effectiveness is to identify the effects that logistical factors may have had on program results. This process helps client and provider understand the outcomes of the program that has taken place and to address logistical factors before further training begins.

Instructor Effectiveness

A third function of evaluation is to determine the effectiveness of the instructor in working with participants and in interacting with client representatives. Instructor evaluation is most important for the workplace language training provider because it serves as a source of information for quality control.

Cost Effectiveness

A final focus of evaluation is to determine whether the provision of workplace language training for employees has been cost effective. Such evaluation looks at the impact of training on the organization as a whole, balancing the cost of training against the benefits that result from improved employee communication skills. Evaluation of a program's cost effectiveness shows the client the degree to which training is a value-added activity whose return on investment warrants its continuation. Cost effectiveness evaluation is also useful for the workplace language training provider, as it documents the value of training in a way that can be used in future marketing efforts.

Practice 9.2: Identify an Effective Evaluation Model

Once the motivation for program evaluation has been defined, the workplace language training provider identifies an evaluation model that will provide the information that client, provider, and any other stakeholders are seeking. The purposes for conducting the evaluation dictate the breadth of the evaluation, for instance, whether it covers only the instructional curriculum and actual training or reaches back to include the needs assessment as well. The goals of evaluation also determine which stakeholders are involved in evaluating the program. The most comprehensive evaluation model will include solicitation of feedback from participants, supervisors and managers, instructors, customers, and any others with whom participants interact in work-related contexts.

When funding for training has been provided by a government or other outside agency, the evaluation model may be dictated in part by agency requirements. For example, if a funding agency requires comparative preprogram and postprogram scores on a standardized assessment of language skill, the administration of the assessment must be included in the evaluation process.

Three commonly used models for evaluation are described here. These are not the only possible models; effective workplace language training providers take an eclectic approach that combines elements of different models to obtain the desired information about a specific program.

The Context, Input, Process, Product Model

A Context, Input, Process, Product (CIPP) evaluation is a comprehensive evaluation that examines all aspects of a workplace language training program, from the initial needs assessment through the development and provision of program content to the final results.

- *Context evaluation* assesses the clarity with which the provider has defined the context within which the program will operate, that is, the need that motivates provision of the program. The evaluator relies on the needs assessment for these data.

- *Input evaluation* assesses the degree to which the program's objectives and procedures corresponded to the program's context as well as how well they represented best practices in the field. The evaluator relies on the performance objectives, instructional curriculum, and instructional materials and activities for these data.

- *Process evaluation* determines the degree to which planned procedures were implemented and identifies any difficulties associated with the implementation of these procedures. Process evaluation is a review of the formative evaluation that took place while the program was in progress. The evaluator relies on a review of program records and on interviews with stakeholders for these data.

- *Product evaluation* determines the degree to which program goals were attained and describes the final outcomes of the program. Product evaluation is also referred to as a summative evaluation. The evaluator relies on a review of performance objectives, end-of-program participant assessments, and program records for these data.

Impact Study Model

An impact study determines how participants and the client organization have benefited from the knowledge the participants acquired from the training program. An impact survey is, in effect, a reverse needs assessment. A needs assessment determines, from a variety of sources, what skills the learners need in order to perform their jobs. An impact survey looks at the learners' performance after they have received training and determines, from a variety of sources, how their performance has changed and whether they can now perform their jobs better. In a traditional evaluation model, the evaluator might ask questions such as the following:

- Did learners master the content of the course? Did they achieve the performance objectives?

- Did program instruction successfully convey the content of the course?

- Did the instructional curriculum, materials, and activities actually fulfill participants' needs?

Because the true test of a program is not how participants perform in class, but rather on how they perform on the job during and after training, impact-oriented questions would direct the focus back to the workplace. Possible questions might include:

- Has the client increased business?

- Has the participants' improved language performance decreased the client's training requirements in other, nonlanguage areas?

- Has the client decreased job turnover and related expenses?

- Has teamwork among employees improved?

- Have participants been able to participate more effectively in internal and external socializing and networking?

Cost-Benefit Analysis/Return on Investment Model

A cost-benefit analysis demonstrates the degree to which a workplace language training program has improved employee productivity and effectiveness. This model defines a successful training program as one for which the cost of training is less than the total financial benefit to the client, such that the program results in a net benefit. The model assumes that all employee work is measurable and can therefore be analyzed in financial terms.

A full cost-benefit analysis includes calculation of the return on investment (ROI)—how much the client will gain as a result of investing in training—and the payback period—how long it will take to recoup the initial investment. Because of the timing and confidentiality of this type of evaluation, the workplace language training provider will need to reply on the cooperation of the client. Accurate calculation of ROI and payback period usually involves variables such as hidden costs of which the provider is not aware.

> ### Case Study 9.2: Community College-Based Vocational Education Program Uses Appropriate Evaluation Model to Restructure Program
>
> A community college in a large urban center in the northeast region of the United States received federal funds to establish a vocational ESL program that would train Spanish and Haitian Creole speakers to become heating, ventilation and air-conditioning (HVAC) technician assistants. Recruitment was successful, and, according to the evaluator, most participants attended class regularly and completed the program on time. However, the program failed to place any of the participants in jobs.
>
> Using the CIPP model, the evaluator reviewed the Needs section of the funding proposal and learned that, although the proposal developer had made the case for a need for HVAC technicians, no case for technician assistants had been made. Because no such position actually existed, no job placements could be found.
>
> Once the problem was recognized, the community college made some curricular changes that modified the program to the broader field of building maintenance. The program was then able to find placements for participants.
>
> Had the evaluator neglected the Context and Input portions of the evaluation, the problem might never have been diagnosed and resolved because an evaluation that only looked at process (formative) and product (summative) data would not have identified the source of the problem.

Practice 9.3: Define and Implement Appropriate Evaluation Mechanisms

Once the provider and the client have selected an evaluation model, the provider develops mechanisms for gathering the desired information from various stakeholders. Mechanisms may include assessments of program participants' learning and their ability to transfer their new knowledge to the workplace; questionnaires that elicit participants' feelings about the program content, the instructional method, the instructor, and other areas of interest; questionnaires or interviews that elicit comments from supervisors and customers regarding improvements they have discerned in participants' job performance; and feedback from instructors and client representatives regarding the logistics of program implementation.

Participant Assessment

A final assessment of participants' classroom learning and transfer of new skills to the workplace builds on the ongoing assessment that has taken place throughout the training program. Effective workplace language training providers avoid pencil-and-paper assessments that ask learners to demonstrate their knowledge of language in ways that are separated from the work context and not relevant to learners' own situations. Instead, they devise ways of assessing participants' progress authentically, in relation to the performance objectives set out in the instructional curriculum. Participants demonstrate that they have mastered the language required for a certain communication task by actually performing the task in a simulated environment. As a result, the participant, the language training provider, and the client all know that the participant can perform that particular task.

In some situations, especially where workplace language training is supported by funding from an outside agency, the workplace language training provider may be required to assess participant progress using a standardized test that does not necessarily reflect the language skill needs of the workplace. In such cases, because the standardized test results do not provide information that is really useful for either the provider or the client, an effective workplace language training provider implements and reports on a more authentic assessment in conjunction with the standardized test.

Interviews and Questionnaires

Brief interviews and short questionnaires give the workplace language training provider an opportunity to collect the often-valuable observations of participants, supervisors, and other stakeholders. The provider selects the interview or questionnaire format, depending on which the client believes will be more efficient and appropriate for its setting.

These interviews and questionnaires parallel those used at the needs assessment stage and, like them, use open-ended questions that encourage thought and the expression of ideas. For example, instead of asking, "Has the participants' ability to do their jobs improved since the training began?," the questionnaire or interviewer might ask, "What changes have you observed? Give an example of improvement." Interviews and questionnaires may also ask respondents to comment (as they are able) on the instructor's teaching style and ability and the logistics of program implementation.

Effective interviews and questionnaires are brief and to the point so that completing them is not a burden. They encourage respondents to suggest alternatives or possible solutions to problems they perceive and therefore serve as a valuable source of information for provider and client alike.

Instructor and Client Feedback

An important part of program evaluation is the collection of feedback from the instructor(s) and from the client on various aspects of the program. This feedback is particularly useful for identifying ways in which the day-to-day working relationship between the client and the provider can be strengthened or improved. The instructor also reports on the effectiveness of the instructional curriculum in meeting client goals and the usefulness of specific materials and activities for helping participants achieve performance objectives.

Effective workplace language training providers generally ask each instructor to provide a written report at the conclusion of a training program. Feedback from the client most often comes in oral form. The input provided by instructor and client is then incorporated with information from interviews, questionnaires, and participant assessments into the provider's overall evaluation of the program.

Case Study 9.3: Provider of Program in Fabric Store Assesses Learning With Tasks That Simulate Real-Life Interactions

To evaluate the workplace language training program for employees of the specialty fabric store described in Case Studies 6.3 and 6.5, the provider assessed participants' learning using communication tasks that simulated actual in-store interactions. The provider also collected responses to questionnaires from the participants and briefly interviewed several of the participants' supervisors and the store personnel manager who had initiated the idea of training in the first place. The instructor for the program provided a written report.

As the manager of the language training company that provided the program was drafting the final written report, the personnel manager called with the news that she had something to add to the evaluation. Customer comment cards were displayed at several locations throughout the store, and one of the store's regular customers had filled one out.

> "When Priva told me that she was taking an English class, we began practicing," the customer wrote. "Every time I come in, she tells me what the class is working on, and we have practice conversations. Priva is very helpful and a wonderful person. Thank you for helping her improve her English so I can get to know her better."

After telling the provider about this comment card, the personnel manager went through the other cards that had come in since the training program began and found three more that provided feedback relevant to the program. The comments on the cards helped the provider and the client achieve a broader understanding of the ways in which workplace language training had had a positive effect on the store's relationship with its customers.

Practice 9.4: Provide a Written Report of Evaluation Results and Recommendations for Future Training

Once evaluation mechanisms have been carried out, the workplace language training provider presents them to the client in a written report. The report begins with a description of the evaluation process. It then outlines the program's goals, the ways in which the goals have been met, and the areas in which further work may be needed. These findings are substantiated by evidence from the evaluation mechanisms that were used to collect data.

Often, the design for the evaluation calls for a draft of the report to be submitted to the concerned parties and discussed with them before the final report is issued. This procedure can help to eliminate mistakes and misunderstandings, thus providing for a more accurate report. In addition, when a written report is required by an external funding agency, review of a draft helps to ensure that the report follows the appropriate format.

In any written report, particularly in one that will be disseminated outside the client organization, confidentiality with respect to the identities of program participants, the identities of those providing feedback, and materials and information proprietary to the client is imperative. In order to preserve confidentiality, a report writer may use pseudonyms and cite statistics rather than individual responses.

Case Study 9.4: Provider Documents Success of Program for Defense Contractor

A large defense contractor in the United States hired a language training firm to provide a program in workplace English for low-level employees. Over the course of a year, the provider conducted three 12-week modules, in each of which 18–20 employees were trained. After the first module, the provider evaluated the training and provided a written report detailing the results of the needs assessment and the ways in which the needs assessment had dictated the performance objectives for program participants. The report then described the program's successes in enabling participants to achieve those performance objectives, as well as some areas in which improvements could be made.

After the second and third modules, the provider submitted similar reports in which it described changes that had been made to the program as a result of the possible improvements outlined in the prior reports, and what the results of those changes had been. The changes resulted in increased ability of participants to meet the performance objectives, and this was reflected in the reports on the second and third modules.

At the end of 1 year, then, the client had a set of three reports that documented how the training program had succeeded and how it had increased its success rate over time. In addition to solidifying an already-strong client-provider relationship, these reports provided major support to the human resources director when she put in a request for an increased training budget for the following year.

▰ Practice 9.5: Conduct Periodic Follow-up

A truly effective workplace language training program has two types of long-term effects. First, there is transfer: whether and how program participants continue to apply in the workplace the content and learning strategies acquired in the classroom. Second, there is impact: whether and how participants' transfer of content and learning strategies to the workplace has positive effects on the organization as a whole. Although transfer and impact can be evaluated in a preliminary way at the conclusion of a training program, their full effect on efficiency, safety, customer relations, and cost containment often cannot be truly measured for some time.

For this reason, effective workplace language training providers prefer to include periodic follow-up in the evaluation process. By continuing to evaluate at 3- or 6-month intervals for a year or two, a provider gains important insights that can help it devise strategies to increase the effectiveness of future training programs. Such periodic follow-up also gives the client an opportunity to review the long-term impact of training and identify other areas or workforce populations for which training could have similar positive effects.

For logistical reasons, such follow-up is often difficult or impossible to carry out. Program participants move to different divisions or different jobs, and client organizations often prefer to evaluate the long-term impact of training as part of their internal assessment process rather than conduct it as a separate exercise. Effective workplace language training providers recognize the reality of such constraints and offer periodic follow-up as a potentially valuable option.

> ### Case Study 9.5: Provider Follows Through as Part of Second Offering of Courses for Financial Services Institution
>
> The contract for the successful program for service representatives at a financial institution described in Case Study 6.1 did not include periodic follow-up after the end-of-program evaluation had taken place. A year after the program's conclusion, however, the client called the provider to request that the program be repeated for a group of newly hired service representatives.
>
> Because the provider had conducted thorough organizational and instructional needs assessments before designing the program, it did not need to carry out such an extensive process again. Instead, the provider used this opportunity to follow up with service representatives who had participated in the program the first time. In individual interviews, the provider asked the first-round participants to describe the ways in which they were applying the knowledge they had gained in the training program and the ways in which they had continued to improve their language skills since the program's conclusion. The provider also obtained input on these same topics from the participants' supervisors.
>
> The information the provider gained from these interviews confirmed the program strengths that had been identified in the end-of-program evaluation. It also shed light on some previously unrecognized areas of need, such as strategies for applying the skills learned for dealing with service calls to other types of calls. As a result, the provider was able to address these needs in the next round of the training program.

Conclusion

Evaluation brings a workplace language training provider and a client full circle in the cycle of training-related activities. The needs assessment process determines the language training needs of program participants and sets them in the larger context of needs and goals of the client organization. The evaluation determines to what extent those needs and goals have been met.

For effective workplace language training providers and their clients, evaluation provides crucial information about a training program's strengths and areas where it could be improved. As evaluation effects closure of one program, therefore, it opens the door to others.

References and Further Reading

Abrams, R. (2000). *The successful business plan* (3rd ed.). Palo Alto, CA: Running 'R' Media.

Belfiore, M., & Burnaby, B. (1995). *Teaching English in the workplace*. Toronto: Pippin.

Bloom, M. R., & Lafleur, B. (1999). *Turning skills into profit: Economic benefits of workplace education programs*. Washington, DC: The Conference Board. Retrieved January 24, 2002, from http://www.conference-board.org/products/researchreports/dpubs.cfm?pubid=R-1247-99-rr

Brieger, N. (1997). *The York Associates teaching business English handbook*. York, England: York Associates.

Burt, M. (1995). *Selling workplace ESL instructional programs* (ERIC Project in Adult Immigrant Education [PAIE] Digest). Washington, DC: National Clearinghouse for ESL Literacy Education/Center for Applied Linguistics.

Burt, M., & Saccomano, M. (1995*). Evaluating workplace ESL instructional programs*. Washington, DC: Project in Adult Immigrant Education/National Clearinghouse for ESL Literacy Education (NCLE)/Center for Applied Linguistics.

Canale, M., & Swain, M. (1980). Theoretical bases of communicative approaches to second language teaching and testing. *Applied Linguistics, 1*(1), 1–47.

Chiswick, B. R. (1996). *The economics of language: The roles of education and labor market outcomes* (Human Capital Development Working Paper Series No. 70). Washington, DC: The World Bank.

Darraugh, B. (Ed.). (1996). *How to write a marketing plan: Practical guidelines for consultants. Info-Line 9514*. Alexandria, VA: American Society for Training and Development.

Dikel, M. F. (Compiler). (2002). *The Riley guide*. Retrieved October 28, 2002, from http://www.rileyguide.com

Douglas, D. (2000). *Assessing languages for specific purposes*. Cambridge: Cambridge University Press.

Dudley-Evans, A., & St. John, M. J. (1996). *Report on business English: A review of research and published teaching materials* (TOEIC Research Report No. 2). Princeton, NJ: The Chauncey Group.

Dudley-Evans, A., & St. John, M. J. (1998). *Developments in ESP: A multi-disciplinary approach*. Cambridge: Cambridge University Press.

Dun & Bradstreet. (1996). *Exporter's encyclopedia*. Murray Hill, NJ: Author.

Ellis, M., & Johnson, C. (1994). *Teaching business English*. Oxford: Oxford University Press.

Fitz-enz, J. (2000). *The ROI of human capital: Measuring the economic value of employee performance*. New York: AMACOM.

Goodstein, L., Nolan, T., & Pfeiffer, J. W. (1993). *Applied strategic planning: How to develop a plan that really works*. New York: McGraw-Hill.

Graves, K. (Ed.). (1996). *Teachers as course developers*. Cambridge: Cambridge University Press.

Hadley, A. O. (1993). *Teaching language in context*. Boston: Heinle & Heinle.

Hayflich, F. P. (1996, Fall). Measuring productivity gains from workplace ESL programs. *Performance in Practice*, 12–13.

Hiebeler, R., Kelly, T. B., & Ketteman, C. (1998). *Best practices: Building your business with customer-focused solutions*. New York: Simon & Schuster.

Hofstede, G.H. (1991). *Cultures and organizations: Software of the mind*. London: McGraw-Hill.

Holtz, H. (1998). *Proven proposal strategies to win more business contracts*. Chicago: Upstart Publishing.

Hutchison, T., & Waters, A. (1989). *English for specific purposes: A learning-centred approach*. Cambridge: Cambridge University Press.

Hymes, D. (1971). Competence and performance in linguistic theory. In R. Huxley & E. Ingram (Eds.), *Language acquisition: Models and methods* (pp. 3–23). London: Academic Press.

Jacoby, S., & McNamara, T. (1999). Locating competence. *English for Specific Purposes*, *18*(3), 213–241.

Kirkpatrick, D. (1998). *Evaluating training programs: The four levels* (2nd ed.). Williston, VT: Berrett-Koehler.

Kirschke, G. (1996/1997, Winter). Adding quality to language training. *Performance in Practice*, 14.

Knowles, M. (1984). *The adult learner: A neglected species* (3rd ed.). Houston, TX: Gulf Publishing.

Krashen, S. (1982). *Principles and practice in second language acquisition*. Oxford: Pergamon.

Lomperis, A. (1999, March). *Exploring cost-benefit analysis for EOP programs*. Paper presented at the 33rd Annual TESOL Convention, New York.

Martin, W., & El Tatawy, M. (1999, March). *Impact survey for an ESP program*. Paper presented at the 33rd Annual TESOL Convention, New York.

Martin, W., & Lomperis, A. (2002). Determining the cost benefits, the return on investment, and the intangible impacts of language programs for development. *TESOL Quarterly, 36*, 399–429.

McDonald, M. (2000). *Marketing plans that work* (2nd ed.). Woburn, MA: Butterworth-Heinemann.

McNamara, T. (1997). Problematising content validity: The Occupational English Test (OET) as a measure of medical communication. *Melbourne Papers in Language Testing, 6*(1), 19–43.

Michigan State University. (2002). *GlobalEDGE*. Retrieved October 28, 2002, from http://globaledge.msu.edu/ibrd/ibrd.asp

National Institute for Literacy. (n.d.). *Equipped for the future*. Retrieved December 6, 2001, from http://www.nifl.gov/lincs/collections/eff/

Nunan , D. (1989). *Designing tasks for the communicative classroom*. Cambridge: Cambridge University Press.

Nunan, D. (1991). *Language teaching methodology*. Englewood Cliffs, NJ: Prentice-Hall.

Oxford, R. (2001). *Integrated skills in the ESL/EFL classroom*. ERIC Digest EDO-FL-01-05. Retrieved October 1, 2002, from http://www.cal.org/ericcll/digest/0105oxford.html

Parry, S. B. (1996). Measuring training's ROI. *Training & Development, 50*, 72–77.

Peyton, J., & Crandall, J. (1995). *Philosophies and approaches in adult ESL literacy instruction*. ERIC Digest EDO-LE-95-06. Retrieved September 6, 2002, from http://www.cal.org/ncle/digests/PEYTON.htm

Phillips, J. (1996). How much is the training worth? *Training & Development, 50*, 20–24.

Savignon, S. (1972). *Communicative competence: An experiment in foreign language teaching*. Philadelphia: Center for Curriculum Development.

Savignon, S. (1983). *Communicative competence: Theory and classroom practice*. Reading, MA: Addison-Wesley.

Savignon, S. (1991). Communicative language teaching: State of the art. *TESOL Quarterly, 25*, 261–277.

Shinkfield, A., & Stufflebeam, D. (1995*). Teacher evaluation: Guide to effective practice*. Norwell, MA: Kluwer.

Stein, S., & Sperazi, L. (1990). *Workplace education in context: A chart comparing traditional and high performance work organizations*. Columbus, OH: ERIC Clearinghouse.

Swales, J. M. (1990). *Genre analysis: English in academic and research settings*. Cambridge: Cambridge University Press.

Trompenaars, A. (1998). *Riding the waves of culture: Understanding cultural diversity in global business*. New York: McGraw-Hill.

Underhill, A. (Ed.). (1994). *The ELT manager's handbook*. Oxford: Heinemann.

United Nations Development Programme. (1998). *United Nations standard products and services code*. Retrieved October 28, 2002, from http://www.un-spsc.net/

United Nations, Interantional Labour Organization. (2002). *International Standard Industrial Classification of all economic activities (ISIC, third revision)* (United Nations Publication St/ESA/STAT/SER.M/4/Rev.3). Geneva, Switzerland: author. Retrieved June 28, 2002, from http://www.ilo.org/public/English/bureau/stat /class/isic.htm.

U.S. Census Bureau. (1997). *North American industry classification system (NAICS)*. Retrieved October 23, 2002, from http://www.census.gov/epcd/www/naics.html

U.S. Department of Labor, Bureau of Labor Statistics. (2002). *Career guide to industries, 2002-03 edition*. Retrieved September 30, 2002, from http://www.bls.gov/oco/cg/home.htm

U.S. Department of Labor, Employment and Training Administration. (n.d.). *America's Labor Market Information System (ALMIS)*. Retrieved September 30, 2002, from http://www.doleta.gov/almis

U.S. Department of Labor, Occupational Safety and Health Administration. (1987). *Standard industrial classification (SIC) codes*. Retrieved July 16, 2002, from http://www.osha.gov/oshstats/sicser.html

Vanett, L. A., & Facer, L. (1994, Spring). Influences from beyond the workplace ESL classroom: The relationship between traditional, transitional, and high performance organizations and workplace ESL teachers. *The CATESOL Journal, 7*, 65–76.

Varner, I., & Beamer, L. (2000). *Intercultural communication in the global workplace*. (2nd ed.). Chicago: Irwin/McGraw Hill.

Vella, J. (1994). *Learning to listen, learning to teach: The power of dialogue in educating adults*. San Francisco: Jossey-Bass.

Vella, J. (2000). *Taking learning to task*. San Francisco: Jossey-Bass.

Vella, J., Berardinelli, P., & Burrow, J. (1998). *How do they know they know?* San Francisco: Jossey-Bass.

Wade, P. A. (1994). *Measuring the impact of training: A practical guide to calculating measurable results*. Irvine, CA: Richard Chang Associates.

Wall Street Journal. (n.d.). *Annual reports service*. Retrieved October 28, 2002, from http://wsjie.ar.wilink.com/cgi-bin/start.pl

West, R. (1994). Needs analysis: State of the art. In R. Howard & G. Brown (Eds.), *Teacher education for LSP* (pp. 68–79). Clevedon, England: Multilingual Matters.

Westerfield, K., & Burt, M. (1996). *Assessing workplace performance problems: A checklist*. Washington, DC: Project in Adult Immigrant Education, National Clearinghouse for ESL Literacy Education (NCLE), Center for Applied Linguistics.

Glossary

chief operating officer (COO): the person who is responsible for managing the daily operations or activities of a company or other organization.

client organization: as used here, the organization, often a business, that receives and usually pays for the workplace language training services.

cold call/ing: calling on a potential client with whom the provider has had no previous direct communication.

communicative competence: a framework that consists of four areas of competency: linguistic, sociolinguistic, discourse, and strategic; used here as the basis for the communicative task/ language analysis.

communicative task/language analysis (CT/LA): taking the communication tasks identified in the initial needs assessment or language audit and breaking them down into performance objectives based on a communicative competence framework.

community-based organization (CBO): a subcategory of nongovernmental organizations (see NGO), operating at a local level.

context analysis: an analysis of the geographic, economic, political, legal, technological, and social factors that affect the business environment.

cost-benefit analysis (CBA): as used here to compare the costs of language training with the benefits or potential benefits of the training.

direct marketing: sending promotional materials to carefully selected potential clients whose industry sector and employees match those identified in the provider's strategic plan.

English for business purposes (EBP). See EPP.

English for occupational purposes (EOP): often used synonymously with workplace language training.

English for professional purposes (EPP): English for individuals working in business, law, government, medicine, or other professions.

English for specific purposes (ESP): EFL/ESL instruction designed around the specific occupational, educational, or social needs of the learners.

genre analysis: the linguistic analysis of a communicative event (written or spoken) that is recognized by an established group or community (e.g., profession or trade) as having a specific purpose and distinguishing features.

human resources (HR): the part of a company or organization that is responsible for recruiting, hiring, training, and maintaining an effective work force; often referred to previously as personnel.

in-house: language training that takes place at the client's site; on-site.

International Association of Teachers of English as a Foreign Language (IATEFL): professional association based in the United Kingdom.

International Standards Organization (ISO) 9000/9001 certification: A set of five universal standards for quality assurance that is accepted in many parts of the world.

language audit: a comprehensive linguistic needs analysis of a department or entire company or organization, involving interviews, shadowing, and examination of documents. The outcome is a formal report with problems prioritized in terms of potential impact. Also referred to as literacy audit in adult workplace literacy.

language training specialist: term used in workplace settings instead of ESL/EFL teacher.

language for occupational purposes (LOP): instruction to address work-related communication needs in any foreign language, not specifically English.

language for specific purposes (LSP): foreign language instruction designed around the specific occupational, educational, or social needs of the learners.

literacy: although traditionally referenced to L1 reading skills, now used broadly to describe a variety of adult basic skills, including reading and writing in the L1, listening, speaking, reading and writing in English (or another target language), basic math and computer skills, and problem-solving and team-work skills.

marketing: as used here, a system for educating and convincing potential clients of the need for a provider's workplace language training services.

networking: making connections, usually for business purposes, through personal acquaintances and professional colleagues.

non-governmental organization (NGO): an international not-for-profit organization that pursues issues of importance to its members through direct action, lobbying or other persuasive tactics (especially in the areas of human rights, poverty, and the environment).

on-site: see in-house.

organizational needs assessment (ONA): the process of gathering information about factors (e.g., an organization's product or service, place of operation, organizational culture, and strategic goals) in a potential client organization that affect the design, delivery, and evaluation of a language training program.

program design: the identified participants, training mode, time frame, physical location and set-up, and staff of a workplace language training program.

provider: as used here, an individual or organization that provides workplace language training services.

present situation analysis (PSA): the current status of workers as it relates to their language proficiency and resulting ability to carry out their job duties.

public relations (PR): the arm of an organization concerned with the organization's image and reputation.

request for proposals (RFP): a formal solicitation requesting bids for a specific product, project, or service.

return on investment (ROI): as used here, an analysis of the direct and indirect financial gains resulting from workplace language training, taking into consideration the costs for the training.

Royal Society of Arts (RSA): British-based organization that includes among its services the training and credentialing of ESL/EFL teachers and teacher trainers.

sponsor: as used here, the organization (or individual) that provides funds for workplace language training; usually a client or governmental agency.

stakeholder: persons or groups interested in and affected by certain decisions.

strategic plan: a plan that outlines a provider's strengths, target markets, goals and objectives, structure, services, and financial condition; used for internal long-range planning and externally to inform potential clients, partners, staff, and investors; also referred to as a business plan.

SWOT analysis: an analysis of an organization's strengths, weaknesses, opportunities, and threats; a framework used in the field of business to describe a structured way for a business or organization to analyze its own potential and develop a strategic plan.

target market: as used here, the specific businesses or organizations to which a provider will market language training services.

target workforce: as used here, the specific group or groups of workers within the client organization who will receive workplace language training.

training division: the part of a company that provides training to its employees.

training groups: term used in workplace settings instead of *class*.

training room: term used in workplace settings instead of *classroom*.

target situation analysis (TSA): as used here, the desired status of the target workforce, with relation to their language proficiency and resulting ability to perform their job duties.

Also Available From TESOL

Academic Writing Programs
Ilona Leki, Editor

Action Research
Julian Edge, Editor

Bilingual Education
Donna Christian and Fred Genesee, Editors

Community Partnerships
Elsa Auerbach, Editor

Content-Based Instruction in Higher Education Settings
JoAnn Crandall and Dorit Kaufman, Editors

Distance-Learning Programs
Lynn E. Henrichsen, Editor

Grammar Teaching in Teacher Education
Dilin Liu and Peter Master, Editors

Intensive English Programs in Postsecondary Settings
Nicholas Dimmitt and Maria Dantas-Whitney, Editors

Interaction and Language Learning
Jill Burton and Charles Clennell, Editors

Internet for English Teaching
Mark Warschauer, Heidi Shetzer, and Christine Meloni

Journal Writing
Jill Burton and Michael Carroll, Editors

Mainstreaming
Effie Cochran

Teacher Education
Karen E. Johnson, Editor

Technology-Enhanced Learning Environments
Elizabeth Hanson-Smith, Editor

For more information, contact
Teachers of English to Speakers of Other Languages, Inc.
700 South Washington Street, Suite 200
Alexandria, Virginia 22314 USA
Tel 703-836-0774 • Fax 703-836-6447 • publications@tesol.org • http://www.tesol.org/